LIBRARY
VERMONT TECHNICAL COLLEGE
RANDOLPH CENTER, VERMONT

D1371376

# The Revolution in Cat Nutrition

## Dr. Jane's Guide—The New Way

LIBRARY
VERMONT TECHNICAL COLLEGE
RANDOLPH CENTER, VERMONT

# The Revolution in Cat Nutrition

❀◈❀◈❀◈❀◈❀◈ ◈❀◈❀◈❀◈❀

## Dr. Jane's Guide—The New Way

❀◈❀◈❀◈❀◈❀◈ ◈❀◈❀◈❀◈❀

### Jane R. Bicks, D.V.M.

*Photography by Terry deRoy Gruber*

*RAWSON ASSOCIATES: New York*

Library of Congress Cataloging-in-Publication Data

Bicks, Jane R.
The revolution in cat nutrition.

Bibliography: p.
Includes index.
1. Cats—Food. 2. Cats. I. Title.
SF447.6.B53 1986 636.8'0852 85-43241
ISBN 0-89256-308-7

Copyright © 1986 by Jane R. Bicks, D.V.M.

All rights reserved

Published simultaneously in Canada by Collier Macmillan Canada, Inc.
Packaged by Rapid Transcript, a division of March Tenth, Inc.
Composition by Folio Graphics Co., Inc.
Designed by Jacques Chazaud
Printed and bound by Fairfield Graphics, Fairfield, Pennsylvania

First Edition

This book is not intended as a substitute for the medical advice of a doctor of veterinary medicine. The reader should regularly consult a veterinarian in matters relating to his/her pet's health and particularly with respect to any symptoms that may require diagnosis or medical attention.

This book is lovingly dedicated to
Croton and Jeddy,
Flotski and Annie,
Bruce,
and
Sufi, of course

# Contents

◆❀◇❀◇❀◇❀

(hepatic) disease. Obesity. Worms (intestinal parasites). Questions and answers about special problems and special diets.

# Acknowledgments

I wish to gratefully express sincere appreciation to all my friends and colleagues whose advice, wisdom, encouragement, and support were invaluable in the preparation of this book, especially James Rapp, Kenneth David Burrows, Thomas Sacklen, D.V.M., Joel Mardan, Peter Mallory, and Hester Mundis.

I would also like to thank the New York Animal Medical Center; the Cornell Feline Health Center; Mark Morris Associates; Michael Garvey, D.V.M.; Thomas Willard, D.V.M., Ph.D.; Ernesto Cabassi, D.V.M.; Lois Guarino; the International Center of Photography; Mary Lou Gregory; Nancy Hass; Helen Carey; Claire Smith; and Ron Van Warmer, for helping make completion of this work possible.

# A Note to the Reader About Nutrient Requirements and Supplement Dosages

✧✿✧✿✧✿✧✿

The National Research Council (NRC) recommended daily requirements included in this book are informational guidelines for prevention of nutritional deficiencies and should not be confused with—or used as—supplement dosages.

When a particular nutrient's requirement falls into a range (2.6 to 7 mg or 5 to 15 IU, for example), the lower number is the *minimum necessary to prevent deficiency* in an ideally average cat (stress-free, physically fit, living in an environment without pollutants and on foods without additives or contaminants); the higher number is a margin of insurance for less than average cats.

Wherever I've suggested supplements and given a range, the lower dosage is what I consider *the minimum needed to achieve a desired beneficial effect;* the higher dosage is the same maximum. (For cats weighing over ten pounds, I recommended the maximum.)

All of my regimens are practical recommendations, though not prescriptions, for enhancing your cat's well-being through improved nutrition. Before starting your pet on any supplement regimen, check with your veterinarian.

# *Preface*

◇❈◇❈◇❈◇❈

How many cats do you think are exactly like yours? None—right?

Right. Like snowflakes, fingerprints, and children—even identical twins—no two are, in *all* respects, *exactly* the same. I'm speaking from over 35,000 cats' worth of experience, but anyone who's ever loved or lived with even one knows this. Unfortunately, knowing that these terrific pets are individuals and treating them as such are two different things—things that far too few owners do.

If there's one thing I can tell you from the vantage point of devoting my entire veterinary career to animal nutrition—really say from the heart and without fear of contradiction—it is this: *Nothing is more important in your cat's life than the right food at the right time.*

And the right time is always now!

People, like cats, are creatures of habit, and habits are difficult to change, especially when food is involved. I say this because despite undisputed acknowledgment that every cat is an individual, thousands and thousands of caring owners continue to feed exactly the same diet to their four-footed companions. They do this regardless of the animal's need, breed, physical condition, age, and environment, unwittingly promoting avoidable problems and denying their pet optimum health.

Let me put it this way: You wouldn't give your ninety-year-old grandmother, who's suffering from acute gastrointestinal problems, a bowl of extra-hot chili just because your nineteen-year-old son thrives on it and that's what you made for dinner, or buy your three-month-old a sirloin steak because it was on sale. You wouldn't serve sugar-frosted chocolate cream pie to a diabetic, hot toddies in the tropics, or steak tartar to a vegetarian. Why? Because you know better.

But how often have you fed dog food to your cat because you got a great buy at the supermarket, or given your tomcat a nightly bowl of milk as a treat, or pampered your finicky eater with a steady diet of prime tuna and raw liver? Statistically: very often. Why? Because you probably don't know better.

But it's not your fault.

Destructive cat diet myths abound, and most of what has been written about feline nutrition is either inaccurate, overly technical, or totally useless on any practical level.

As a consultant to the ASPCA and pet food companies, and from the questions repeatedly asked at my numerous lectures over the years, I've found that what people don't know—or think they don't *need* to know—about feeding cats is what most often undermines their cats' health. So, realizing that a complete, comprehensive cat nutrition guide—with *specific* preventive and therapeutic information and instructions for all regimens and dosages—has been long over-due, I resolved to write it. As with all resolutions, this was easier said than done. But fortified by my lifelong love and dedication to the well-being of these wonderful creatures, I did it!

The primary purpose of this book is to help you help your cat, at any age and under all circumstances, enjoy a better life through superior and specialized nutrition. To enable you to accomplish this with minimum effort and time, I've provided fast-fix feeding tips, as well as meal plans, recipes, and remedies for maximizing health, preventing illness, and modifying your pet's behavior. The mainstay of this path to fitness is my New-Life Diet: *a sensible and scientific feeding program designed specifically to produce visible health and be-havior improvements in virtually any cat within thirty days.*

Since I firmly believe that every cat is unique, I have individu-alized, to the best degree possible, care, diet, and vitamin-mineral requirements for the different needs of different breeds, for kittens, older cats, mothers-to-be, finicky eaters, overeaters, plant eaters, inside cats, outside cats, aggressive cats, shy cats, and others.

I've also included sections on common and uncommon ailments (how to prevent, recognize, and treat them), emergency procedures, administering medication, giving your pet home health checks (what to look for and why), feeding in a multi-pet household, cat "health foods," and herbal remedies. And I've included a special inside guide to commercial foods that tells you what to look for—and look out for—on pet food labels, so that you get the best nutritional (and economical) brand for your particular cat.

I've done my best to stress the long-term life- and money-saving benefits of preventive cat nutrition. I've kept explanations simple and all diet-restructuring suggestions flexible enough to fit your pet, your budget, and your life-style, because I want you to discover how remarkably easy it is to feed your cat to fabulous fitness.

It goes without saying that no book is a replacement for a veterinarian's personal care when that is what's called for. My hope is that I've provided enough information to prevent calling for it often and unnecessarily.

Jane R. Bicks, D.V.M.

# PART ONE

# Feeding
# to Win

◇❀◇❀◇❀◇

# *The Love-Life-Diet Connection*

❖❀❀◇❀◇❀◇❀

## My Love-Life-Diet Discovery

*How a sick cat from Brooklyn turned my life around*

Though I'd lived with animals all my life, preferred them to playmates of my own species, and from childhood had a special love for cats, I hadn't planned on becoming a veterinarian.

I hadn't planned on falling in love with a desperately ill Maine coon kitten from Brooklyn.

I hadn't planned on a lot of things that were going to change my life.

*Luck and Fate:* I was a student at that time, living alone in New York, and studying to be a pharmacist. On my way home from class one day, I was walking past an abandoned lot when something stopped me: a faint, pathetically faint, mewling.

I knew at once that there was a cat in trouble, but not until I reached her, pushed aside the weeds, and knelt down beside this pitifully emaciated, obviously dehydrated little orphan coon cat did I realize how serious the trouble was. She was

*3*

feverish, her eyes watery and barely open. Her natural black coat with its chest bib of white (barely discernible) was a lifeless, rat-colored gray, matted with excrement and dirt.

The symptoms were frighteningly familiar and heart-breakingly classic: distemper.

I petted her tentatively. Weak as she was, she somehow managed to raise her head and look at me; it was a look of gratitude and a plea for help that I've never forgotten.

Without hesitating, I picked her up and raced to the nearest phone booth. Setting her down gently on my sweater, I grabbed the yellow pages and called the first veterinarian listed. I explained the situation and the kitten's symptoms, and to my dismay was told that nothing could be done and not to bring her in. I got the same response from the next vet I phoned . . . and the next . . . and the next. . . . It wasn't until I reached "Veterinary Clinics" that a vet finally agreed to see us.

Distemper was accepted routinely in those days—and by many today—as virtually incurable for cats; for kittens it was a death sentence.

The little orphan trying to push her nose against my arm couldn't have been more than two months old.

Wrapping her in my sweater, I ran home for my car, set her tiny limp body on my lap, and named her Tashi, crooning it as we headed for the clinic.

I felt like crying when we reached the clinic. It was wedged between a butcher shop and a laundromat in a rundown section of Brooklyn. From the outside the place looked more like a flophouse than a veterinary hospital. The waiting room didn't look much better.

Neither did Tashi.

The doctor, Dr. Goldberg, led us into the examining room immediately. Before I'd even put Tashi on the table, he had a syringe in his hand, told me to hold her steady, and gave her an injection. Then he examined her thoroughly, nose to tail, shaking his head sadly throughout the entire procedure.

"Will she. . . ?" I couldn't even ask the question.

"You must force her to eat," he said. It was a command, not advice. "She needs liquids, good nourishment, and food that will harden her stool." He wrote out a short list and handed it to me.

"But—but what about medication? Antibiotics?"

"The last thing this animal needs in her condition is to lose more nutrients! What I've already given her to prevent further dehydration and infection was a risk, not a cure." He sighed. "I'm sorry. What upsets me is, now that vets know that drugs can do many things, they often forget that these are not always the *right* things to do."

How true, I thought, recalling a test I'd taken recently on the revised indications and contraindications for established medications. But how frustrating. I stared at the list Dr. Goldberg had given me.

He pressed my fingers closed around it. "There is nothing more I can do."

Saying thank you numbly, I cradled Tashi in my arms and asked what I owed.

"You are a student, yes?"

I nodded.

"You owe me nothing."

"Nothing?" Stunned and grateful, I thanked him again. I had no idea at that time how very much I owed him.

As I turned to leave, he said, "Bring her back tomorrow if she's still alive."

*Night Shift:* I spent nearly that entire evening hand-feeding Tashi at regular intervals, giving her teaspoons of professional cat food (discussed in chapter 4) blended with pureed, cooked chicken livers and rice and what I calculated from my basic pharmaceutical and nutrition training would be a balanced amount of pediatric vitamins and minerals for her age and size. Using an eyedropper, I was also able to give her a mixture of diluted evaporated milk, honey, and raw egg yolk.

Now, for a healthy kitten this would have been royal treatment beyond belief: constant attention, specially prepared, finger-fed gourmet food, and all accompanied by delicious milk and honey.

Unfortunately, Tashi was anything but a healthy kitten. Having distemper disease—known for causing cats to refuse to eat or drink and therefore unwittingly starve to death—she seemed to view my nutritional ministrations as cruel and unusual punishment. This broke my heart, yet I couldn't really blame her.

What I've euphemistically described as hand-feeding was actually force-feeding (which does have a sort of cruel-and-unusual-punishment ring to it). Nonetheless (as explained in chapter 7), it is a technique that's often required for a cat's well-being. In Tashi's case it was a matter of life or death. And I was determined not to settle for the latter.

I ignored her feeble protests and sustained myself by repeating, "All's fair in love and war" and that this was war and I was in love.

Somewhere around 5 A.M. battle fatigue set in.

Tashi, for all my ministrations, had evidenced no improvement. Exhausted, disheartened, and unconsolably sad, I fell asleep beside her. I didn't want to think about waking up.

Three hours later, I had no choice: two white-tipped paws were patting my nose, a black tail was tickling my chin, and a warm furry head was rubbing against my chest. I was euphoric. She'd made it through the night.

I couldn't wait to call Dr. Goldberg.

That afternoon, when he'd completed examining Tashi, Dr. Goldberg once again shook his head sadly and said exactly what he'd said the day before, and would continue to say for the next week: "Bring her in tomorrow if she's still alive."

I did—and she became more alive with each passing day.

*An Ending and a Beginning:* Within four weeks the scrawny Brooklyn back-lot orphan—now savoring my specially prepared meals and thriving—blossomed into a five-pound bundle of boundless energy and remarkable beauty, and, along with Dr. Goldberg, changed the course of my life forever: I no longer wanted to be a pharmacist—I was determined to be a veterinarian.

Tashi and I enjoyed many wonderful years together, both here and in Italy, where I graduated *summa cum laude* from veterinary school. Her special combination of feline mischief and magic was unique, and though I've loved and lived with many cats, I never will or can forget her.

Nor will or can I ever forget Dr. Goldberg, that wonderful man who always insisted I owed him nothing, but whose unconventional forays into the curative and preventive powers of nutrients have been—and still are—a continuing inspiration for dedicating my veterinary career to animal nutrition.

## Tails That Told More than Stories

*There's no pussyfooting around nutrition when you're catering to cats.*

As a veterinarian at the County Animal Clinic in Yonkers, New York, I was one of a fortunate few privileged to have daily contact and consultation with some of the nation's foremost board-certified specialists in all fields of animal medicine. It was an incomparable opportunity for gaining firsthand, state-of-the-art veterinary experience, opening vast areas of knowledge to me, particularly about felines, and was essentially responsible for my realization that most sick cats are victims of uneducated owners or casualties of ill-equipped boarding facilities.

Convinced of this, Dr. Richard Jackimer (also from the County Animal Clinic) and veterinary technician Chris Thedings joined me in opening the Cat Hilt-Inn. It was the first four-star feline boarding facility owned and operated by registered veterinarians, totally dedicated to maximizing the health of all cat residents through nutrition.

My enthusiasm for the endeavor was boundless. And though it cost me nights of sleep, days of frustration, and incalculable hours of work, what I learned from our boarders and their owners was priceless.

## The Mysteriously Balding Siamese Siblings

Maja and Raja were two six-year-old Siamese cats who had never been boarded before. Their owners had been called to England to settle some family affairs and would be unable to return for at least a month. They were distraught about leaving their "babies."

I was distraught *looking* at their "babies."

Though the animals' health forms (required for all cats we boarded) appeared to be in order, Maja and Raja certainly did not. Both were virtually hairless and had chests so slack and saggy they resembled kangaroo pouches. Talk about an undynamic duo! This pair exhibited about as much vitality as a couple of garden slugs. Something was definitely wrong.

I had nothing to go on but a hunch, so I decided to play it: I asked what the cats were being fed.

"Only the best!" I was told indignantly.

"Only the best what?" I asked, soft-pedaling my tone of voice so as not to appear dubious.

"Ground steak and raw liver."

"And . . . ?" I prompted, waiting for them to continue.

"And nothing else," was their defiant reply.

My hunch had been right. Maja and Raja were suffering from a royal case of all-meat syndrome, a completely unbalanced diet that was not only denying but depleting them of essential nutrients (particularly B vitamins and carbohydrates), causing them increasing loss of energy and general deteriorating health.

I requested permission to change Maja and Raja's diet to a balanced-formula cat food. Well . . . you would have thought

I'd asked to feed them cyanide! I was told in no uncertain terms that their "babies" would never eat it.

It took me awhile to get the owners' approval, but after I assured them that the new diet would be given on a carefully supervised trial basis and that the cats would never go hungry, they reluctantly consented. (They were convinced, I'm sure, that they were never going to see Maja and Raja again.) I promised to send a letter every week, keeping them informed of their pets' condition.

They left teary-eyed and forlorn.

That night I gave Maja and Raja each a bowl of dry, professional, fixed-formula food, high in recuperative and body-building nutrients. Let me just say, for animals who "would never eat cat food," those two did a superb job of faking it. They devoured every morsel and continued to do so for all the days that followed.

Within one week their hair began to grow back; within two, their coats were fine-textured and glossy, and with daily exercise their kangaroo pouches were beginning to firm into muscles. By the third week they were looking sleek and growing more energetic daily. By the end of their four-week stay, they were the Hilt-Inn's most glamorous, mischievous, and talkative couple (if it was time for dinner, they let me know it!).

When their owners returned, they viewed Maja and Raja's transformation as nothing less than a miracle, even though I explained that it was nothing more than nutrition. They didn't care. Maja and Raja were signed on as regular weekend boarders.

MORAL: *Food that is "only the best" for people can be just about the worst for cats.*

## The Cat with Invisible Legs

She was an orange tabby named Goldilocks and looked as if she'd just eaten three bears. Obese? This cat made Garfield look anorectic. She was so fat that when she stood (which was in itself a remarkable feat), her legs were invisible, totally hidden by her enormous body.

Since Goldilocks also had a rash that extended from mid-back to tail, had cowlicks of matted fur, and reeked of unpleasant fecal odor, I immediately asked what she was being fed.

"Well, I like to treat her kind of special," replied the owner. "She has a tendency to be frightened and pants a lot, so I guess I sort of spoil her." She then proceeded to tell me that she not only left three varieties of dry food available for Goldilocks at all times, but gave her breakfast leftovers, luncheon leftovers, a can of 9 Lives for dinner, and a bedtime snack of whatever pastry, pudding, or ice cream happened to be around (judging from the owner's own more than ample figure, I suspected these were rarely *not* around). This woman was not spoiling her cat, she was killing it. Goldilocks' frightened panting was due, I felt certain, to excess fat around the heart.

"She's quite a bit overweight," I said as tactfully as possible.

"Goldie?" The woman shook her head. "She's just a big cat; eats everything I give her." No doubt about that, I thought, but felt it inappropriate to say so at the time.

As the woman rose to leave, it took several moments for her to lift Goldilocks and plump all twenty-seven pounds of her into my lap. "You know," she said, slightly winded, "maybe Goldie could lose a little weight."

That's what I wanted to hear.

The first night with Goldilocks was the hardest. I started her on Feline r/d, a professional reducing diet cat food that supplied all necessary nutrients and included enough bulk fiber to appease her hunger without adding calories.

I weighed her every day, and by the end of the first week she had lost two pounds and was beginning to groom herself (which was almost physically impossible at her former size, especially with that enormous belly). After losing two more pounds the following week, Goldilocks really got into grooming. The rash on her back began to clear up, because she was using her tongue regularly to clear away dead epithelial cells, stimulate her oil glands, and distribute her natural oils. Her cowlicks disappeared and her fur began to shine.

Within three weeks she was visibly slimmer, more alert, more active, and odor-free, since she now could easily clean her anal-genital area.

The owner was ecstatic when she saw the change in Goldilocks' appearance, and promised she would keep up the food and grooming regimen I'd begun. I told her to brush Goldilocks daily with a soft (natural bristle) brush, weigh her daily, and keep her on the reducing diet for at least another month or two, then switch to a good alternative food.

She obviously followed my instructions, because when I saw them some time later, Goldilocks was in grand condition. She was still chubby—and most likely always would be—but she was outgoing, healthy, and strutting on four now very visible legs. Probably not coincidentally, the owner had dropped some weight and looked much better, too.

MORAL: *Cats given too many treats get unjust desserts.*

## The Scaredy-Cat Solution

Oscar was a slim, lethargic, dull gray, pin-striped, domestic shorthair around six years old. His owner had brought him in for boarding because she was upset about his increasing timidity, aversion to socializing, and general apathy. She believed Oscar had a psychological problem.

When I asked why she believed this (since the cat had been heard and seen playing while she was at work), she explained that several years before, Oscar, who'd always been essentially an indoor cat (with limited yard privileges in summer), had witnessed a neighbor's cat kill a bird and eat it. She was convinced that this had traumatized Oscar and was the cause of her formerly outgoing, active pet's current introverted behavior.

I found it difficult to share her conviction. For one cat to see another kill a bird could hardly be construed as traumatic, particularly since hunting and prey-catching are innate in felines, even if they've never been outside. Whatever Oscar's problem, that wasn't it.

I looked over his admittance form and saw nothing unusual. But I had learned from past experience that much of what wasn't written turned out to be what was most informative. And more often than not—as I was discovering daily—that information had to do with diet. I asked about Oscar's.

"Well, he always has dry food available," his owner told me, "but he gets a can of food for breakfast before I go to work, then another can for dinner when I come home, and then before I go to bed I give him, you know, some sort of treat. A muffin, a piece of pie, cookies, whatever's around. And he eats all of it."

I was surprised and slightly baffled. That amount of food was excessive, even for the most active cat, and yet Oscar was not overweight. A former extrovert, he had now regressed to curling up behind chairs and under the bed. The pieces didn't seem to fit—but I had more than a sneaking suspicion that they would. I asked her to leave Oscar with me for the week.

I put Oscar on a normal twice-a-day feeding schedule, and within three days discovered through a routine fecal examination that his ravenous appetite and lack of weight gain were due to tapeworms. His assumed timidity, aversion to socializing, and lethargy had come about simply because his owner was serving him a feline equivalent of three Thanksgiving dinners daily! No wonder he didn't care to do more than just lie down and curl up. Who would? Who could?

I explained this to his owner, though she was still reluctant to concede that Oscar's problem was not psychological until she came to pick him up and he obliterated all doubt by literally bounding into her arms. After a week of having been fed just two quality meals a day—and in spite of not yet being completely worm-free—his timidity and apathy were gone. High-spirited, extroverted Oscar was back to normal and raring to go.

MORAL: *Never overfeed a cat with anything but love.*

## Making Your Own Discoveries

*Your lack of curiosity could be harmful to your cat.*

Once a cat has become established as an integral part of your home and your life, it's not uncommon for both of you to take each other for granted, especially where feeding is concerned. This is perfectly understandable. After all, it's a routine with seductive mutual benefits.

For kitty: same food, same time, same place; dependable.

For you: can opener, cup; no thought required.

Unfortunately, these mutual benefits, as with most seductive things, can be risky and have regrettable, unforeseen consequences.

Just because your cat isn't visibly ill doesn't mean that he or she is healthy. I say this not to frighten you, but to impress upon you the amazing fact that the majority of all common cat ailments are preventable and curable through early symptom recognition and the immediate implementation of enhanced immunity nutrition. (See "Preventive Nutrition Tactics" in chapter 3.)

### *Avoiding Nutritional Cat-astrophes*

The following list has been designed as a flashing caution light—a signal to look more carefully at what you have (or have not) been feeding your cat.

NOTE: This list is not all-inclusive, nor is it—or any other in this book—meant as license for you to play veterinarian. Its purpose is to alert you to possible *nutritional* distress signals that, if recognized early, can be rectified, thereby averting numerous potential health problems for your pet.)

IMPORTANT: *Many of these symptoms can also be indications of already-present serious diseases. Because of this, I urge you to double-check them in chapter 7, where they are detailed separately under "Symptoms Can Be Serious."*

## DISTRESS SIGNAL: *Vomiting*

| POSSIBLE DIET PROBLEM | FINDING HELP |
| --- | --- |
| Feeding a food that is not nutritionally balanced for your cat's age or breed. | See chapters 5 and 6 for your cat's special requirements. |
| Cat is eating too quickly, perhaps because of the presence of other pets or being fed in a busy, stressful area. | See chapter 3 for tips on how to avoid mealtime mistakes. |
| Food is too cold, causing gastrointestinal upset. | See chapter 3 for suggestions on proper preparation. |
| Food has been kept too long and spoiled. Leftovers unfit for you are just as unfit for your cat. | See chapter 4 for how—and how long—to store cat food. |
| Hunger. This type of vomiting—usually of a yellow, frothy consistency—can occur when your cat's stomach is empty. | See chapter 3 for how to adjust feeding schedules. |
| Vitamin B deficiency, commonly caused by poor-quality commercial foods, all raw-meat diets, or stress, but easily rectified by supplements or adding debittered brewer's yeast mixed with ½ teaspoon wheat germ to food. | See chapter 4 for vitamin-deficient cat foods; see chapter 2 for other B-rich additions to your cat's diet. |
| Eating grass, most likely due to empty stomach—possibly due to overeating, sometimes nutrient deficiency. | See chapter 3 for why cats eat plants. |

| POSSIBLE DIET PROBLEM | FINDING HELP |
|---|---|
| Poor teeth and gums, causing gulping of food. | See chapter 4 for how to prevent tooth decay; see chapter 5 for tips on feeding toothless cats. |
| Hair balls. | See chapter 7 for prevention and remedies. |
| Worms and intestinal parasites. | See chapter 11 for prevention and remedies. |
| Too much vitamin C. | See chapter 2 for needs and supplement cautions. |
| FUS (feline urologic syndrome) possibly caused by too much magnesium in diet. | See chapter 11 for disease prevention, symptoms, and recommended diet. |
| Constipation (what won't go one way will come out another). | See "Carbohydrates" in chapter 2 for diet preventives and cures. |
| Ingestion of foreign objects. | See chapter 7 for remedies. |

**DISTRESS SIGNAL:** *Excessive Shedding*
*(including scarce or brittle hair)*

| POSSIBLE DIET PROBLEM | FINDING HELP |
|---|---|
| Nutrient deficiency in food, most likely inadequate protein, fatty acids, and vitamins A, E, and B complex. | See chapter 10 for balanced and complete diet; see chapter 2 for good natural sources that supply these nutrients. |

| POSSIBLE DIET PROBLEM | FINDING HELP |
| --- | --- |
| All-meat syndrome, a raw-meat diet providing insufficient amounts of nutrients—calcium, in particular—for adequate food metabolization. | See chapter 3 for common feeding mistakes; see chapter 2 for nutrition requirements. |
| Worms and intestinal parasites. | See chapter 11 for prevention and remedies. |
| All-fish diet, can cause vitamin E deficiency condition called steatitis. | See chapter 3 for feeding mistakes; see chapter 2 for nutrition requirements. |

## DISTRESS SIGNAL: *Dry, Flaking, or Oily Skin*

| POSSIBLE DIET PROBLEM | FINDING HELP |
| --- | --- |
| Wrong or insufficient protein, fats, or vitamins and minerals in diet. | See chapter 2 for good and bad types of fats for cats; supplements; and foods to avoid. |

## DISTRESS SIGNAL: *Lack of Muscle Tone*

| POSSIBLE DIET PROBLEM | FINDING HELP |
| --- | --- |
| Calcium deficiency, particularly if muscle around sternum (breastbone) is flaccid. | See chapter 7 for instructions on checking for muscle tone; see chapter 2 for preventing calcium deficiency. |
| Obesity; can't feel muscle mass—only fat—along cat's backbone and rib cage. | See chapter 11 for dietary prevention and cure. |

| POSSIBLE DIET PROBLEM | FINDING HELP |
| --- | --- |
| Undernourishment; particularly if you feel no muscle, only backbone. | See chapter 11 for proper way to fatten a thin cat. |
| Inadequate utilization of nutrients or improper food; insufficient exercise, particularly in indoor cats. | See chapters 6 and 9 for breeds' special needs and characteristics. |

## DISTRESS SIGNAL: *Short Whiskers*

| POSSIBLE DIET PROBLEM | FINDING HELP |
| --- | --- |
| Inadequate protein quality or intake, insufficient nutrients to utilize available protein. | See chapter 2 for protein needs, why certain deficiencies occur, and how these can be prevented and rectified through diet; see chapters 5 and 6 for special age and breed needs. |

## DISTRESS SIGNAL: *Split Nails*

| POSSIBLE DIET PROBLEM | FINDING HELP |
| --- | --- |
| Insufficient intake of nutrients, such as vitamin A, vitamin E, and iodine. | See chapter 2 for vitamin and mineral needs and avoiding deficiencies; see chapter 4 for evaluating pet foods. |

### DISTRESS SIGNAL: *Runny Eyes (Mucous Discharge)*

POSSIBLE DIET PROBLEM

FINDING HELP

Insufficient vitamin A in diet, or addition of too many polyunsaturated fats (which can inhibit vitamin A usefulness).

See chapter 3 for preventive measures; see chapter 2 for proper use of fats for cats.

### DISTRESS SIGNAL: *Unhealthy (Cracked or Broken) Pads*

POSSIBLE DIET PROBLEM

FINDING HELP

Not enough dietary fat or protein, or incorrect proportion of nutrients in food.

See chapter 2 for proper nutrient requirements.

### DISTRESS SIGNAL: *Diarrhea*

POSSIBLE DIET PROBLEM

FINDING HELP

Overeating.

See "Obesity" in chapter 11 for how to control your pet's eating.

Change in diet.

See chapter 10 for how to ease your cat into a new food regimen.

Deficiency in vitamins A and E, other fat-soluble vitamins, and nutrients necessary for utilization.

See chapter 2 for fat requirements and prevention of oxidation.

Rancid or decayed food.

See chapter 4 for how—and how long—to keep cat food.

| POSSIBLE DIET PROBLEM | FINDING HELP |
|---|---|
| Large doses of vitamin C. | See chapter 2 for needs and supplement cautions. |
| Insufficient natural bran or fiber in diet. | See chapter 4 for well-balanced cat foods; see "Carbohydrates" in chapter 2 for how to supplement. |
| Worms or intestinal parasites. | See chapter 11 for prevention and remedies. |
| Raw egg white in diet; can cause biotin deficiency. | See chapter 3 for avoiding mealtime mistakes. |
| Too many carbohydrates in diet. | See chapter 2 for nutrient needs and cautions. |
| Allergy to single food ingredient; all-meat or all-fish diet. | See chapter 3 for common feeding mistakes and diet myths. |

## DISTRESS SIGNAL: *Crust Around Eyes or Mouth*

| POSSIBLE DIET PROBLEM | FINDING HELP |
|---|---|
| Zinc, biotin, and/or niacin deficiency. | See chapter 2 for vitamin and mineral needs and best food supplements. |

## DISTRESS SIGNAL: *Sores That Don't Heal*

| POSSIBLE DIET PROBLEM | FINDING HELP |
|---|---|
| Insufficient fat-soluble vitamins, protein, zinc, and vitamin C being metabolized in diet. | See chapter 2 for how to make sure the nutrients your cat is getting are being used effectively. |

## DISTRESS SIGNAL: *Pale Mucous Membranes (Gums or Eyelids)*

POSSIBLE DIET PROBLEM

FINDING HELP

Inadequate intake of protein, vitamins, necessary trace minerals, and particularly iron, biotin, and copper.

See chapter 7 for how to examine your cat; see chapter 4 for foods that are nutritionally balanced.

## DISTRESS SIGNAL: *Bad Breath*

POSSIBLE DIET PROBLEM

FINDING HELP

Deficiency of B vitamins in diet.

See chapter 2 for prevention of vitamin loss and vitamin B-rich foods.

Excess gas due to poor digestion of food.

See chapter 4 for guide to cat food pluses and minuses.

Worms or intestinal parasites.

See chapter 11 for prevention and remedies.

Gum or tooth decay, often caused by lack of dry food needed to keep teeth clean.

See chapter 4 for cat foods that can help maintain dental health.

## DISTRESS SIGNAL: *Lack of Appetite*

POSSIBLE DIET PROBLEM

FINDING HELP

Diet change.

See chapter 1 for how to ease cat into accepting new food.

Multinutrient deficiency in current food, particularly A, E, and B vitamins.

See chapter 2 for nutrition requirements; see "Anorexia" in chapter 11 for foods to stimulate appetite.

**DISTRESS SIGNAL:** *Attitude (Listlessness and Apathy)*

POSSIBLE DIET PROBLEM        FINDING HELP

Increasing malnutrition due to either poor-quality cat food or nutrient inadequacy in home-cooked meals.

See chapter 10 for a good restorative diet; see chapters 5 and 10 for recipes that are nutritionally balanced for your cat.

## Questions and Answers About the Love-Life-Diet Connection

### JEKYLL AND HYDE EATING

*My three-year-old male cat, Rocky (a neutered domestic shorthair), is sort of a Jekyll and Hyde eater. He'll devour half a can of Kal Kan's Mealtime in the morning, then won't even touch the other half when I serve it at night, though if I open a can of another food, he'll down it with gusto. Sometimes he'll eat a food only at night, sometimes just in the morning—and sometimes not at all. I know the food isn't spoiled because I refrigerate it. Have you ever heard of this sort of food neurosis? And is it curable?*

I've heard of it: cold-food neurosis. Happily, it's not really a neurosis and is readily curable. Rocky, not unlike many cats, just doesn't like cold food. (This isn't an unwise preference on his part, since cold food often causes gastric disturbances in cats.) I'd suggest warming the refrigerated portions of his meals to room temperature. Either add a tablespoon of hot water or broth, mix, then test with your finger; warm the can in hot water as you would a baby bottle; or remove the contents to a microwave dish and warm. *Never reheat the food.* This destroys the nutrients and will make the meal worthless for feeding.

One alternative (though it could be costly) is to buy smaller, one-portion cans; another is to feed Rocky a quality low-magne-sium-content dry food. (See chapters 4 and 11 for suggestions.)

## FLAKY CAT

*I have a black shorthaired house cat with a dandruff problem. She's been checked for worms and has none. I bathe and brush her regularly, but it doesn't seem to help. I tried adding bacon grease to her food, but it made her vomit, so I stopped. Any suggestions?*

Quite a few. First, hold off on the bathing (shampoos can wash away your cat's natural oils, and unless there is a real need to bathe a cat, don't), but do keep up the brushing. This stimulates oil glands and distributes natural oils. Use a soft bristle brush. Since your cat stays indoors, her skin is more prone to dryness. In winter a humidifier can help, but adjusting her diet is your best all-year-round preventive.

Make sure she is getting an adequate amount of *high-quality* protein and essential fatty acids—those that cannot be made in the body and must be obtained from food. (See chapter 2.) She also needs ample amounts of vitamin E to prevent oxidation of these fats and to ensure the effectiveness of other fat-soluble vitamins such as A, D, and K as well as B complex.

Avoid feeding all-fish foods, which are high in unsaturated fats that can decrease vitamin E efficiency, and chlorinated water, if possible. Raw egg yolk—*not white*—is a good dietary addition, as is any quality fatty-acid supplement (such as Borden's Mirracoat or Linatone).

# Nutrition ABC's for C-A-T-S

❖❀❖❀❖❀❖❀

## Why Human and Cat Nutritional Needs Differ

*Our brains are similar, but our
dietary needs are not.*

Except for our larger frontal lobes and speech and memory-association capacities, cats and humans have virtually identically structured brains. This is a fine bit of trivia, but useless—and often harmful—when it comes to eating, feeding, and nutrition.

*Your Cat Is Not a Little Furry Person.* No matter how human your cat behaves, whether it licks your ear like a lover, demands hors d'oeuvres at cocktail parties, can be easily insulted, has opinions about your friends, or cons you into giving up your place on the couch, its digestive system, metabolism, and nutrient needs are uniquely feline.

## Differences That Make the Difference

• Protein requirements for cats are higher than those for humans.

• Cats, unlike humans (or dogs and other mammals), *cannot* store excess protein and must replenish their supply through daily dietary intake.

• Cats cannot be vegetarians and thrive; they have short intestines—whereas humans have long ones—and therefore are unable to utilize vegetable protein effectively. Moreover, cats cannot convert beta-carotene, present in plants, to vitamin A as we can, and must consume preformed vitamin A, which can be obtained only from animal tissues.

• Growing kittens need about one third more protein per pound than human infants do.

• An eleven-pound cat needs approximately the same minimum daily thirty grams of protein that a forty-four pound four- to six-year-old child does!

• Cats must consume the preformed arachidonic fatty acid found only in animal tissues, since, unlike humans, they cannot convert linoleic to arachidonic fatty acid. (see "Fats" below).

• Cats can have diets consisting of up to 64 percent fat (and I mean the kind of saturated fat that doctors tell us to cut down on or die) and live healthier and more vigorous lives than the majority of nutrition-conscious humans.

• Magnesium dosages that help humans prevent kidney stones can potentiate them in cats, along with FUS (feline urologic syndrome) and other bladder and kidney ailments.

• Humans can use the amino acid tryptophan to manufacture the B vitamin niacin, but cats cannot and therefore need more niacin in their diet.

• Certain food preservatives (such as benzoic acid) that are harmless to humans can be toxic to cats.

• And, to top it off, our ages aren't the same. (See chapter 5 for comparisons.)

## Protein: The Number One Cat Nutrient

### UNDERSTANDING WHAT IT IS

• The foremost dietary structural material for all mammals in general and cats in particular.

• A combination of amino acids—the building blocks of protein—that form thousands of different proteins (which perform specific functions) and are also the end product of protein digestion.

• The *essential* amino acids cats must obtain from foods are:

| | |
|---|---|
| *arginine* | *phenylalanine* |
| *histidine* | *taurine* |
| *isoleucine* | *threonine* |
| *leucine* | *tryptophan* |
| *lysine* | *valine* |
| *methionine* | |

### HOW PROTEIN CAN BENEFIT YOUR CAT

• Helps growth, maintenance, and repair of all animals' tissue.

• Promotes and sustains a high-powered immunity system.

• Fuels the active feline metabolism.

• Aids in developing and strengthening a cat's thousands of springlike muscles. (*Building* muscles still requires exercise.)

### HOW MUCH IS NEEDED?

Adult cats need 3 g per pound of body weight daily. Kittens need 8.6 g per pound of body weight daily.

REMEMBER: *Cats cannot store excess protein and must replenish their supply every day through food.*

### BEST HIGH-QUALITY PROTEIN SOURCES FOR YOUR CAT

Lean muscle meat (beef, lamb, turkey, chicken); fish (cooked); egg yolk (no raw white); whole egg (cooked); organ meats (kidney, liver); whole milk protein (casein); whole cereal grains (wheat germ, cornmeal).

### Protein Deficiency Symptoms and Diseases
Abdomen distension (swollen belly), hair loss, lethargy.

### My Advice for Owners
Whoever says "You can't get too much of a good thing," does not know enough about cat nutrition. As important a nutrient as protein is, it *should not* be your cat's entire diet. *All-meat or all-fish diets cause more harm than health!* In fact, even though pregnant and lactating cats as well as growing kittens need increased protein in their diets, feeding them only meat can cause calcium deficiencies.

Remember that the protein you do feed your cat should be a *complete* protein; that is, it should contain all the essential amino acids. In other words, animal protein.

Always bear in mind that the better the protein quality— "quality" meaning its high biological value (BV) and efficient usability by the body—the less your cat needs. Protein percentages on labels are often misleading and can undermine your pet's health if read incorrectly. (See chapter 6.)

## Carbohydrates

### Understanding What They Are
• They are nutrients derived from plants.
• They include starches, sugars, cereals, and cellulose (grain fiber).

### How Carbohydrates Can Benefit Your Cat
As long as your cat is getting a proper protein/fat ratio in its diet, the right carbohydrates can serve as a backup energy source.

Cellulose fiber, such as bran, can:
• provide necessary bulk to stimulate intestinal movement and prevent constipation;

• help cleanse intestine walls of digested food residue (chyme);

• form a gel in the gastrointestinal tract that will regulate the absorption of nutrients, particularly water and minerals, and aid in preventing diarrhea.

### How Much Is Needed?

Cats have no standard requirements for carbohydrates, but for optimal health they need at least one—*processed* rice, corn, or wheat (not whole)—and preferably two for backup energy.

Not more than 10 to 15 percent of a cat's daily diet should consist of carbohydrates.

Amount of fiber (bran) is best determined by an individual cat's needs. (Too little: constipation; too much: diarrhea.)

### Best High-Quality Carbohydrate Sources for Your Cat

*For backup energy:* processed corn, wheat, or rice. *For fiber:* wheat bran, beet pulp, vegetables.

### Carbohydrate Deficiency Symptoms and Diseases

None known, though chronic constipation could indicate a deficiency of fiber.

### My Advice for Owners

Many cats enjoy raw vegetables and fruits (my Siamese, Croton, adores alfalfa sprouts, lettuce, and cantaloupe!) and benefit from the vitamins and minerals they contain. These vegetarian indulgences are fine as long as your cat's primary diet has an ample protein/fat content.

*Vegetarians and dieters take heart:* If your cat is into veggies, there's nothing wrong with having your pet join you in a salad once or twice a month. Indoor cats love it! A modified Caesar salad (see recipe in chapter 10) is a nutritious change-of-pace treat for kitty, a great diet incentive for you, and a fabulous way to use up those anchovies that would otherwise go to waste.

Raw starches can often cause diarrhea in cats, which is why grains and legumes should be cooked and ground, so that the carbohydrates they contain can be digested.

If you want the benefits of fiber for your cat, wheat or rice bran will provide the kind you're looking for.

## Fats

### UNDERSTANDING WHAT THEY ARE

• Fats are the most concentrated source of a cat's dietary energy (fat contains approximately twice the calories of either carbohydrates or protein).

• Fats are composed of fatty acids; the ones of prime importance for your cat are linoleic, linolenic, and arachidonic. These unsaturated fatty acids are called *essential* because they cannot be manufactured by the cat's body and must be obtained through diet. Linoleic and linolenic can come from vegetable sources, but arachidonic acid *must be obtained from animal fat*.

• They carry Vitamins A, D, E, and K (fat-soluble vitamins) around the body and enable them to be properly utilized.

• Their quality and type are more important than their percentage in your cat's diet.

### HOW FATS CAN BENEFIT YOUR CAT

• Make foods more palatable.

• Supply needed energy, particularly during periods of growth or stress.

• Promote healthy skin and shiny coat.

• Aid in feline fitness by regulating glandular activity and making calcium readily available to cells.

• Help improve immunity in tissue.

• Assist in thermal regulation of body temperature.

## How Much Is Needed?

A balanced dry food should not contain *less* than 15 percent fat.

The average house cat's daily diet should contain 20 to 40 percent fat.

As much as 64 percent of your cat's caloric needs can be given in the form of fat, unless obesity is a problem. (See chapter 11.)

The NRC (National Research Council) requirement is only 9 percent, but that's because they have not taken into consideration the type of fat, your type of cat, or the amount of food you're feeding daily. Additionally, their evaluation is based solely on dry food.

### Best High-Quality Fat Sources for Your Cat

*Soft* animal fat (chicken fat, bacon grease), butter.

### Fat Deficiency Symptoms and Diseases

Dry skin, dull or brittle coat, frequent illness (such as colds), hair loss with crusting, lethargy.

### My Advice for Owners

I suggest you familiarize yourself with the differences between soft (short-chain) fats and hard (long-chain) fats before adding any to your pet's diet. Soft fats are essentially those that melt easily (poultry fat, butter, and bacon grease, for example). These are extremely beneficial to your cat because they are readily digested and able to supply energy as well as carry vitamins A and E, choline, and other nutrients quickly to where they're needed.

Hard fats, such as tallow (the kind of thick, white fat you find around the outside of a steak), though highly palatable, are not as easily digested and utilized.

Because of their availability and lower cost, hard fats are generally used in cat foods. If properly processed and cleanly rendered, they are fine sources of arachidonic acid, which cats cannot synthesize and must obtain from animal fats. Unfortunately, most generic and many supermarket-label foods often use inferior quality, improperly processed hard fats which are not easily digestible and, in fact, are frequently nonutilizable.

Unusable fat usually goes one of five places: (1) It's vomited up; (2) it's stored in the liver, killing cells, and could eventually cause fatty liver disease; (3) it becomes adipose tissue (tummy fat); (4) it goes out the oil glands (you have one greasy cat); or (5) it passes through the stool. So when you think of adding fat to your cat's diet, do your pet a favor and think soft.

Do not confuse soft fats (see above) with oils, particularly vegetable oils (such as corn and safflower oil). Though they have twice the fatty acids of soft fats, *they're not the right ones!* Though some veterinarians recommend wheat germ oil (which is all right, but not the best for cats because of its lack of arachidonic fatty acid), I feel they do it more to please the owner than to benefit the cat.

Be aware that all dry cat foods containing fat have some preservative, even if the product claims to be "all natural." The manufacturer might not have added anything, but the fat supplier had to preserve the fat with something . . . and that *something* doesn't have to be on the label. (See chapter 4.) This is misleading, but better than the alternative—rancid fats make very sick cats.

## Vitamins

Vitamins are organic substances found in minute quantities in natural food and are essential to normal life-functioning in all animals. With few exceptions they cannot be manufactured internally and must be obtained through diet or supplements.

## Vitamin A

### UNDERSTANDING WHAT IT IS

• A fat-soluble vitamin that requires sufficient fats and minerals in order for proper absorption to take place.

• Though there are two forms of this vitamin—preformed vitamin A (called retinol and found only in foods of animal origin) and provitamin A (called beta-carotene and found primarily in foods of plant origin)—cats, unlike humans and dogs, cannot convert beta-carotene to vitamin A and must obtain it from retinol (an animal source).

• As a fat-soluble vitamin, it can be stored in the cat's body. Because of this, it doesn't need daily replenishment, and an oversupply (for instance, a dietary lavishing of too much beef liver upon your pet) can cause an unhealthy buildup and hypervitaminosis (symptoms: reduced, painful, or crippling neck movement, abnormal walking, muscle degeneration).

### HOW VITAMIN A CAN BENEFIT YOUR CAT

• Increases immunity and aids in prevention of bladder, respiratory, and other infections.

• Promotes growth, skin and coat health, fertility, and muscle coordination.

• Helps pituitary gland function.

• Improves vision, hearing, and digestion.

• Provides protection against toxic chemicals in foods and water.

### HOW MUCH IS NEEDED?

The recommended minimum daily allowance is 1,000 to 3,000 IU for an average healthy cat.

### BEST HIGH-QUALITY VITAMIN A SOURCES FOR YOUR CAT

Liver, kidneys, egg yolk (no uncooked white), butter, fish-liver oil.

### Vitamin A Deficiency Symptoms and Diseases

Loss of appetite (anorexia), muscle atrophy, weight loss, dull or brittle coat, scaly hairless patches on skin, overgrowth of the cornea, conjunctivitis, retinal degeneration, intolerance of light (photophobia), resistance to petting or handling, impaired fertility. In tomcats: testicular atrophy. In kittens: weakness, irregular muscle coordination (ataxia), tremors, and paralysis.

### My Advice for Owners

Vitamin A is vital in the diet of every cat, so be sure it's listed on the label of whatever food you're feeding. And while you're reading that label, check to see that the food *doesn't* contain sodium nitrite! This additive, present in many cat foods, can deplete vitamin A. (See chapter 4.)

If you're thinking of supplementing your pet's diet, liver is a good choice, but *don't overdo it!* (Too much vitamin A is as dangerous for your cat as too little.) I'd suggest that if you're going to add it to your cat's regular food, liver should not make up more than 25 percent of the meal. If you're going to serve it as a meal in itself, I'd recommend not doing so more than three times a week, unless your veterinarian has specifically advised you to do so.

Cod-liver oil, though not a great fat supplement because of its lack of arachidonic acid, is a fine source of vitamin A. Adding just one-fourth teaspoon of it to your pet's meal three to five times a week should be adequate to keep vitamin A levels intact. *If you suspect a serious deficiency, contact your veterinarian.*

Never give your cat mineral oil as a vitamin supplement! Mineral oil can deplete the body of vitamins A, D, E, and K, calcium, and phosphorus.

To be sure your cat is getting the most from vitamin A, whatever you're feeding should also include B complex vitamins, vitamins D and E, calcium, and zinc.

## Vitamin B₁ (Thiamine)

### UNDERSTANDING WHAT IT IS

• A water-soluble member of the B complex; like the others, any excess is excreted instead of being stored in the cat's body, and must be replaced daily.

• Cooking heat, food-processing methods, extended storage, sulfa drugs, air, and water destroy its potency.

• Works synergistically: is more effective when taken together with other B vitamins, particularly $B_2$ (riboflavin) and $B_6$ (pyridoxine), than alone.

• Cats have an exceptionally high requirement for B complex vitamins.

### HOW VITAMIN B₁ CAN BENEFIT YOUR CAT

• Stimulates appetite.

• Improves mental attitude, behavior, and intelligence.

• Keeps nervous system, muscles, and heart functioning normally.

• Helps maintain optimal feline fitness.

### HOW MUCH IS NEEDED?

The recommended minimum daily allowance is 0.2 to 1.5 mg for an average healthy cat. (More is required during lactation, illness, and growth and stress periods.)

### BEST HIGH-QUALITY VITAMIN B₁ SOURCES FOR YOUR CAT

Brewer's yeast, pork, bran.

### VITAMIN B₁ DEFICIENCY SYMPTOMS AND DISEASES

Loss of appetite (anorexia), loss of muscular coordination (ataxia), vomiting, weight loss, heart dysfunction, convulsions, paralysis.

## My Advice for Owners

Let me start by telling you to stop doing something: feeding your cat raw fish. Many, such as carp and herring, contain an element in their tissues that prevents the absorption of thiamine, which can result in your pet's developing a vitamin $B_1$ deficiency.

Because cats have a great need for thiamine (as well as the other B complex vitamins), mixing brewer's yeast into their food on a regular basis—providing FUS isn't a problem—is a good idea. Not only can this help ensure that they're really getting their daily requirement but it can help keep them flea-free! Thiamine (ample in brewer's yeast) seems to give cats some imperceptible scent that repels fleas. (It takes at least a month for this internal repellent to become effective, so don't be disheartened if at first the fleas succeed; thiamine will win—for most cats—eventually.)

If your cat is on antibiotics, recovering from surgery, or under any sort of stress, the need for thiamine (and all B vitamins) is increased. You can get B complex supplements or Borden's Bene Bac (which contains all the B vitamins as well as vitamins A, D, E, and acidophilus) at pet food stores or from your veterinarian.

## Vitamin $B_2$ (Riboflavin)

### Understanding What It Is

• Another water-soluble member of the B complex, which cannot be stored in your cat's body and needs to be replaced regularly through diet.

• Easily absorbed and easily excreted.

• Depending on cat's needs or deficiencies, excretion may be accompanied by protein loss.

• *Not* destroyed by heat or oxidation (as thiamine is), but does dissolve in cooking liquids and is destroyed by light.

### How Vitamin B₂ Can Benefit Your Cat
- Helps prevent eye problems and cataracts.
- Aids in metabolization of carbohydrates, protein, and fat (essential for the release of energy from food).
- Acts as a preventive for dry, cracking skin.

### How Much Is Needed?
The recommended minimum daily allowance is 0.2 to 1.5 mg for an average healthy cat. (More is needed during lactation, illness, and stress or growth periods, and for cats on a high-fat diet.)

### Best High-Quality Vitamin B₂ Sources for Your Cat
Liver, kidney, cottage cheese, cooked fish, brewer's yeast.

### Vitamin B₂ Deficiency Symptoms and Diseases
Loss of appetite (anorexia), weight loss, cataracts, hair loss (alopecia). In tomcats: testicular atrophy.

### My Advice for Owners
If your pet is under stress (a move, an operation, an illness), riboflavin—along with the other B complex vitamins and vitamin C—is a wise diet supplement. When adding any of the natural sources that I've mentioned above, don't go overboard. These foods should constitute no more than 25 percent of your cat's regular meal, unless your veterinarian has advised you otherwise.

CAUTION: If your cat has cancer and is taking an antineoplastic (anticancer) medication, an excess of vitamin B₂ can reduce the drug's effectiveness. Check with your veterinarian before making any diet alterations.

## Vitamin B₃ (Niacin, Niacinamide, Nicotinic Acid)

### UNDERSTANDING WHAT IT IS

• Another water-soluble member of the B complex, and needs to be replaced in your cat's diet daily.

• Easily destroyed by cooking, food processing, sulfa drugs, and water.

• Unlike humans and dogs, cats cannot convert the amino acid tryptophan (found in turkey, meat, cottage cheese) to form niacin, making them completely dependent on dietary intake.

• Necessary for proper synthesis of insulin, sex hormones, cortisone, and thyroxine (the hormone produced by the thyroid gland).

### HOW NIACIN CAN BENEFIT YOUR CAT

• Increases energy through effectively metabolizing protein and fat.

• Helps prevent negative behavior by promoting a healthy nervous system.

• Aids in eliminating and preventing mouth sores and bad breath.

• Alleviates gastrointestinal problems and keeps digestive system healthy.

### HOW MUCH IS NEEDED?

The recommended minimum daily allowance is 2.6 to 7 mg for an average healthy cat. (More is needed during lactation, illness, and stress periods.)

CAUTION: Do not give your cat a niacin supplement without a veterinarian's advice. It can cause itching and great discomfort to your pet.

### BEST HIGH-QUALITY NIACIN SOURCES FOR YOUR CAT

Liver, heart, kidney, brewer's yeast, poultry white meat, wheat germ, egg yolk (no uncooked white).

### NIACIN DEFICIENCY SYMPTOMS AND DISEASES

Diarrhea, mouth ulcers, thick saliva, bad breath, fever. In kittens and young cats: loss of appetite (anorexia), weight loss, lethargy, dangerously increased susceptibility to respiratory infections.

### MY ADVICE FOR OWNERS

If your cat is taking antibiotics, you might want to add some niacin-rich food to the animal's regular diet. Brewer's yeast (unless FUS is a problem), sprinkled on and mixed in the food, is the easiest way to sneak it into a finicky eater's diet.

Most cats, unlike most children, respond enthusiastically to liver. Since it is a fine source of niacin (and all B vitamins), serving it as a single-meal treat one to three times weekly or adding it to your pet's regular food (being sure that it constitutes no more than 25 percent of the cat's ration) is a good way to ensure niacin sufficiency. The same can be done with any of the foods listed above.

*Do not* give your cat any of your own niacin supplements. Most come in 50 to 1,000 mg form, much too large a dose for little felines.

## Vitamin B₅ (Pantothenic Acid, Calcium Pantothenate, Panthenol)

### UNDERSTANDING WHAT IT IS

• A high-standing member of the water-soluble B complex, needing daily dietary replacement, and particularly important in the production of protective antibodies.

• Necessary for the proper function of the adrenal glands (situated outside each kidney and essential for producing cortisone, hormones, and the healthy regulation of virtually all feline metabolic functions).

• Easily destroyed by canning, heat, food-processing techniques, and sulfa drugs.

• An essential antistress vitamin.

### How Vitamin B$_5$ Can Benefit Your Cat

- Prevents and fights infection by building antibodies.
- Alleviates stress and combats effects of toxins.
- Aids in providing protection and relief from allergies.
- Helps in healing wounds.
- Minimizes adverse side effects of antibiotics.

### How Much Is Needed?

The recommended minimum daily allowance is 0.5 to 1.5 mg for an average healthy cat. (More is required during illness and stress periods.)

### Best High-Quality Vitamin B$_5$ Sources for Your Cat

Liver, kidney, egg yolk (no uncooked white), wheat germ, bran, chicken, green vegetables (see salad recipe in chapter 10).

### Vitamin B$_5$ Deficiency Symptoms and Diseases

Weight loss, fatty liver disease, susceptibility to allergies.

### My Advice for Owners

Vitamins B$_5$, B$_6$, and B$_9$, otherwise known as pantothenic acid, pyridoxine, and folic acid, are the SWAT team protectors of your cat's immune system. Essential contributors to antibody production, these three Bs should be included in your pet's diet daily. (They work better together than alone.)

If you're planning on spaying or neutering your cat, increasing the amount of vitamin B$_5$ in the animal's diet before and after the operation can prevent adverse stress reactions and speed recovery.

A cat that's prone to or suffers from allergies often has inadequate pantothenic acid and vitamin C production. This can and should be rectified through improved diet or vitamin supplementation. (See cautions for supplementing vitamin C below.)

## Vitamin B₆ (Pyridoxine)

### UNDERSTANDING WHAT IT IS

• A superstar in the water-soluble B complex, though equally excretable and requiring daily replenishment.

• Essential for the proper metabolization of a cat's ingested protein and fat—as well as for effective absorption of vitamin $B_{12}$ (cobalamin).

• Indispensable for the production of healthy red blood cells and antibodies.

• Easily destroyed by long storage, food-processing techniques, canning, sterilization, cooking, and water.

### HOW VITAMIN B₆ CAN BENEFIT YOUR CAT

• Aids in optimal assimilation of protein and fat.

• Fortifies the immune system (particularly when accompanied by pantothenic and folic acids).

• Improves behavior by preventing many nervous disorders.

• Helps in alleviating skin problems.

• Enables proper utilization of essential minerals.

### HOW MUCH IS NEEDED?

The recommended minimum daily allowance is 0.2 to 1.5 mg for an average healthy cat. (More is required during lactation, illness, and stress and growth periods.)

### BEST HIGH-QUALITY VITAMIN B₆ SOURCES FOR YOUR CAT

Brewer's yeast, wheat germ, wheat bran, organ meats (liver, kidney, heart), beef, egg yolk (no uncooked white), cantaloupe.

### VITAMIN B₆ DEFICIENCY SYMPTOMS AND DISEASES

Weight loss, inhibited growth, anemia, kidney disease, convulsions, dry or crusting skin.

## My Advice for Owners

Few vitamins are more important for high-protein consumers than $B_6$. Because cats rank among the highest protein consumers, the need for ample amounts of this vitamin is unquestionable. Since this vitamin is destroyed easily by storage and food processing, I'd suggest that if you're currently feeding your pet generic or low-quality food, you definitely get some quality pyridoxine into the cat's diet. Pronto!

You'll find, once again, that brewer's yeast covers a lot of bases: It's inexpensive, contains all the necessary B vitamins (which, when working synergistically, are much more effective), and is easily made palatable when mixed with your cat's regular fare. Unfortunately, brewer's yeast also contains 0.17 percent magnesium, and is therefore not recommended for cats with FUS problems.

If your cat is being treated with drugs for arthritis, ask your vet if the medication contains penicillamine. If it does, your pet needs extra vitamin $B_6$. (Depending upon the treatment, you might want to ask your veterinarian about a professional vitamin supplement.)

CAUTION: Vitamin $B_6$ can reduce a diabetic cat's need for insulin. To avoid a low blood sugar reaction, consult your veterinarian before making any dietary changes. (See chapter 11.)

## Vitamin $B_9$ (Folic Acid, Folacin, Vitamin M)

### Understanding What It Is

• Yet another water-soluble member of the B complex, and essential to the healthy development of all parts of a cat's body.

• Necessary for the effectiveness of other stress-fighting and antibody-building B vitamins. (If not present, effectiveness of other B vitamins is decreased.)

• Needed for the utilization of amino acids and the formation of red blood cells.

• Can be destroyed by food processing, heat, water, sunlight, sulfa drugs, and storage at room temperatures for extended periods.

### How Folic Acid Can Benefit Your Cat
- Helps maintain a powerful immune system.
- Aids in protecting against intestinal parasites and food poisoning.
- Promotes growth and health of the fetus.
- Improves lactation.
- Stimulates the appetite.

### How Much Is Needed?
Though no official minimum daily allowance has been set, 10 to 25 mcg is suggested for an average healthy cat. (More is required during pregnancy, lactation, stress, and during antibiotic treatment.)

### Best High-Quality Folic Acid Sources for Your Cat
Brewer's yeast, organ meats (liver, kidney, heart), egg yolk (no uncooked white), cantaloupe, dark green leafy vegetables (see salad recipe in chapter 10).

### Folic Acid Deficiency Symptoms and Diseases
Anemia, weight loss. In kittens: impaired growth.

### My Advice for Owners
A good B complex will give your cat a sufficient amount of folic acid, as it is only required in minute amounts (micrograms). If your pet is ill or fighting off an illness, more folic acid is required, but unless a special supplement is advised by your veterinarian, I'd suggest simply augmenting your cat's diet with any of the multiple B complex foods listed above. Keep the 25 percent rule in mind. By changing only one quarter of your cat's regular meal, you're more likely to enhance the animal's health and less likely to incur feline wrath.

If your cat is pregnant, lactating, or on antibiotics, an

increase in folic acid is recommended. Since, at times like these, the last thing you want is to take a chance on your cat's rejecting food (which some finicky eaters will do if there's the least alteration in diet), I'd suggest asking your vet for a supplement.

## Vitamin B₁₂ (Cobalamin)

### UNDERSTANDING WHAT IT IS
• A water-soluble member of the B complex that, like folic acid, is quite effective in small doses.
• The only vitamin that also contains essential mineral elements.
• On commercial food labels it is often listed as the additive cobalamin concentrate or cyanocabalamin.
• Its absorption can be impaired by a poorly functioning thyroid gland.
• It is most effective when accompanied by foods containing all the B complex vitamins, as well as vitamins A, E, and C. Additionally, it must combine with calcium during absorption to be of benefit to the animal's body.

### HOW VITAMIN B₁₂ CAN BENEFIT YOUR CAT
• Improves the immune system and prevents anemia.
• Aids in effective metabolization of protein, fat, and carbohydrates.
• Alleviates behavior problems by promoting a healthy nervous sytem.
• Promotes growth and increases appetite in kittens and young cats.

### HOW MUCH IS NEEDED?
No standard daily allowance has been established for cats, but a minimum of 5 mcg is recommended.

### BEST HIGH-QUALITY VITAMIN B₁₂ SOURCES FOR YOUR CAT
Liver and other animal organ meats, beef, pork, cheese, egg yolk (no uncooked white).

### VITAMIN B$_{12}$ DEFICIENCY SYMPTOMS AND DISEASES
Anemia, impaired growth, susceptibility to infection.

### MY ADVICE FOR OWNERS

Like folic acid, a little vitamin B$_{12}$ goes a long way. In fact, it works best with folic acid (along with the rest of the B complex and vitamins A, E, and C) and can be a real energizer for lethargic cats.

An imbalanced diet—one that's low in vitamin B$_1$ and high in folic acid (which I've seen happen when owners decide they want their cats to become vegetarians)—can not only cause a vitamin B$_{12}$ deficiency but hide it, for quite a while, from all but the most extensive (and expensive) medical tests.

Steer clear of all store-bought B$_{12}$ supplements, unless they are prescribed by your veterinarian.

## Biotin (Vitamin H, Coenzyme R)

### UNDERSTANDING WHAT IT IS

• A water-soluble member of the B complex that is required by cats in small amounts and aids in its synthesis of vitamin C.

• Necessary for effective metabolism of protein, fat, and carbohydrates.

• Avidin (a protein found in raw egg whites) can prevent its absorption and usefulness in the body.

• Works synergistically with riboflavin, niacin, pyridoxine, and vitamin A in keeping a cat's skin and coat healthy.

• Food-processing techniques, water, sulfa drugs, and raw egg white can destroy its effectiveness.

### HOW BIOTIN CAN BENEFIT YOUR CAT

• Helps prevent hair loss, dermatitis, and other skin conditions.

• Aids in maintaining proper thyroid and adrenal gland function.

• Promotes a healthy nervous system.

• Assists in providing optimal metabolization of food.

### How Much Is Needed?

The recommended minimum daily allowance is 15 mcg for an average healthy cat.

### Best High-Quality Biotin Sources for Your Cat

Brewer's yeast, egg yolk (no uncooked white), beef liver, kidney, unpolished rice (ground).

### Biotin Deficiency Symptoms and Diseases

Runny eyes, mouth and nose discharge, loss of appetite (anorexia), severe weight loss, scaly patches of face, bloody diarrhea.

### My Advice for Owners

Don't give your cat raw egg white. Use just the yolk, or cook the egg. This will prevent a lot of nutritional problems and allow your pet to benefit from the biotin content in the meals you're feeding.

Your cat's need for biotin is increased during antibiotic or sulfa drug therapy, but a prepared supplement is rarely necessary. Good B complex additions to the diet will usually provide a sufficient amount of this nutrient. (If the treatment is for an extended period time and your pet is evidencing any signs of deficiency, consult your vet for a supplement.)

## Choline and Inositol

### Understanding What They Are

• Water-soluble members of the B complex that work together in metabolizing fats and cholesterol for effective utilization.

• Lipotropics (fat emulsifiers) that, when combined, form lecithin.

### How Choline and Inositol Benefit Your Cat

• Help the liver eliminate poisons and drugs from the body.

- Enhance nerve impulse transmission and improve memory.
- Modify excitability and produce a calming effect.

### How Much is Needed?
For an average healthy cat the recommended minimum daily allowance of choline is 50 to 100 mg; for inositol it is 10 to 25 mg.

### Best High-Quality Choline and Inositol Sources for Your Cat
Egg yolk (no uncooked white), organ meats, wheat germ, brewer's yeast, green leafy vegetables, cantaloupe.

### Choline and Inositol Deficiency Symptoms and Diseases
Possibly fatty liver disease (see chapter 11); rough, scaly skin (eczema).

### My Advice for Owners
Since most foods containing B complex vitamins also contain choline and inositol, there is no need for special or additional supplementation. I say this on the assumption that by now you realize how important B complex vitamins are to a cat's well-being. (If you don't, go back and reread this chapter.)

Perhaps the one exception to choline and inositol supplementation might be if it is absolutely essential to maximize your cat's vitamin E intake, and you don't want to risk overdosing your pet. Choline and inositol are safe and natural vitamin E potentiators.

CAUTION: Choline is contraindicated for cats with liver disease.

## Vitamin C (Ascorbic Acid, Cevitamic Acid)

### Understanding What It Is
- A water-soluble vitamin that cats can synthesize in their

bodies (in the liver), but in amounts too small to provide significant health benefits or immune protection.

• Excreted in urine, it is used up rapidly during periods of stress, growth, and illness and must be replaced through dietary sources.

• Cooking, heat, light, water, exposure to air, and certain medications destroy vitamin C.

• Essential in forming collagen (the primary constituent of connective tissue, bone, and cartilage), and necessary for the growth and repair of a cat's teeth, gums, bones, blood vessels, and tissue cells.

• Needed for the animal's proper absorption of iron.

• On food labels it often appears as the additive ascorbic acid or sodium ascorbate.

### How Vitamin C Can Benefit Your Cat

• Improves the immune system and aids in preventing many types of viral and bacterial infections.

• Alleviates allergies (can inhibit release of histamine).

• Provides protection from toxins (either in food or in the environment).

• Helps build strong teeth, gums, and limbs, and retards deterioration of them as the animal ages.

• Aids in preventing and curing cystitis and feline urinary problems.

• Helps counteract side effects of steroids (often used to reduce itching or increase appetite in animals) that interfere with collagen formation.

• Can relieve joint pain.

• Acts as a preventive for cancer and feline leukemia.

• Helps in treatment of respiratory and liver diseases.

• Speeds up healing after surgery.

### How Much Is Needed?

No minimum daily allowance has yet been established for cats, since they are capable of manufacturing the vitamin—

not, however, in amounts needed for either disease prevention or general well-being—but 50 to 100 mg is advised. (During illness, vitamin C synthesis is impaired and 100 to 300 mg daily is recommended.)

### BEST HIGH-QUALITY VITAMIN C SOURCES FOR YOUR CAT
Tomato juice, cantaloupe, leafy vegetables, rhubarb.

### VITAMIN C DEFICIENCY SYMPTOMS AND DISEASES
Inflammation of the gums (gingivitis), joint and muscle pain, fatigue, brittle bones (all possible symptoms of sub-clinical scurvy).

### MY ADVICE FOR OWNERS
For an effective immune system, cats definitely need more vitamin C than the small amount their bodies produce. This is especially true for indoor cats. Outdoor cats can supplement their supply of vitamin C by hunting or eating their prey, which, if it's a mouse, has this vitamin in large supply. These outdoor hunters might not devour all of what they kill, but they'll almost always eat the liver (where ascorbic acid is made) and the adrenal glands (where it is stored) and some muscle tissue (which also contains the vitamin).

Stress of any kind (illness, a new pet in the home, travel, and so on) calls for more vitamin C than most cats can produce to combat it successfully. This lowers their resistance, making them more vulnerable to infections (viral and bacterial) and disease, in effect leaving them with an immune system that's not even worth its name.

Most cat foods are not fortified with vitamin C, despite increasing evidence that it's invaluable to feline well-being, so it's a good idea to supplement your pet's diet. Though natural vitamin C is found primarily in fruits and vegetables (not, admittedly, feline favorites), many cats do enjoy the taste of tomato juice. (Don't knock it if your cat hasn't tried it.) Just a little added to your pet's food each day can help keep urine acidic and aid in preventing cystitis and other common urinary ailments.

Cat vitamin C supplements are available at pet stores or can be obtained from your veterinarian. Always follow the directions on the label. (Too much can cause diarrhea, among other unpleasant side effects.)

IMPORTANT: *Before starting any supplement regimen, check with your veterinarian.*

I don't generally recommend giving cats human vitamin C supplements. Yes, ascorbic acid for humans is the same for cats, but unless you're certain about how much to give and how to go about giving it, unnecessary problems can result. A pill that's easy for you to take might be too large for your cat, get stuck in the animal's throat, and, if it's ascorbic acid, can burn your cat's esophagus. (Before giving your cat any pill, coat it with some butter. The butter will mask bitterness and allow the pill to slide down easily. See chapter 7 for tips on how to administer medications.)

If you're determined to share your vitamin C supply with your pet, you're better off pounding or grinding the pill into a powder, mixing it with some butter, chicken fat, or bacon grease, and then mixing that into your cat's food. (Use moist, canned food and stir it well, so that your cat won't be able to smell or taste the ascorbic acid.) Supplemental dosage for an average adult cat is 100 mg daily.

By the way, city cats and cats who live with smokers need extra vitamin C.

## Vitamin D (the "Sunshine Vitamin," Calciferol, Viosterol, Ergosterol)

### UNDERSTANDING WHAT IT IS

• A fat-soluble vitamin that cats obtain primarily from sunlight. (Ultraviolet rays, acting on the animal's skin oils, produce the vitamin, which is then absorbed into the body.)

• When obtained through food (essentially, fish oils), it is absorbed with fats through the intestinal walls.

• Can be stored in the body and does not require daily replenishment. (An oversupply can cause hypervitaminosis D: an uneven distribution of calcium in the bones, abnormal teeth, a dangerous hardening of soft tissue in lungs, kidneys, heart, and blood vessels.)

• On food labels it is often listed as the additive calciferol, ergocalciferol, or cholecalciferol.

• Necessary for the proper utilization of calcium and phosphorus.

### How Vitamin D Can Benefit Your Cat
• Promotes strong bones and teeth.

### How Much Is Needed?
The recommended minimum daily allowance is 50 to 100 IU for an average healthy cat.

### Best High-Quality Vitamin D Sources for Your Cat
Sunlight, egg yolk (no uncooked white), fish oils.

### Vitamin D Deficiency Symptoms and Diseases
Malformation of bones and teeth, weak muscles and joints (rickets).

### My Advice for Owners
Beware of supplementing this vitamin unless you've been instructed to do so by your vet. Though it's true that an insufficient supply of vitamin D can impede your cat's absorption of needed calcium, the chances of feline vitamin D deficiency are rare.

Do not use cod-liver oil (or any other fish oil) as a routine daily dietary supplement. If you're under the impression that doing this is the way to improve your cat's coat or strengthen bones and teeth, you're wrong. Moreover, you're seriously endangering your pet's health by inviting hypervitaminosis D.

### *Vitamin E (Tocopherol)*

#### UNDERSTANDING WHAT IT IS

• A fat-soluble vitamin that, unlike some others (A, D, and K), is stored only for a relatively short time in the body.

• An important antioxidant, preventing oxidation of fat compounds, vitamin A, selenium, some vitamin C, and other nutrients.

• Destroyed by food processing, extremes in temperature, iron, chlorine, and mineral oil.

• Often appears on food labels as the additive alpha tocopheryl acetate, alpha tocopheryl concentrate, or alpha tocopheryl acid succinate.

#### HOW VITAMIN E CAN BENEFIT YOUR CAT

• Strengthens the immune system.

• Provides protection against environmental pollutants and toxins.

• Retards cellular aging, boosts endurance, and promotes rejuvenative behavior.

• Aids in prevention of steatitis (caused by all-fish diets).

• Helps in curing skin problems.

• Enhances fertility.

• Enables other nutrients to function more effectively.

#### HOW MUCH IS NEEDED?

The recommended minimum daily allowance is 5 to 15 IU for an average healthy cat. (More is needed when the cat's diet is high in polyunsaturated fats, found in canned tuna fish.)

#### BEST HIGH-QUALITY VITAMIN E SOURCES FOR YOUR CAT

Wheat germ, broccoli, spinach, egg yolk (no uncooked white), enriched flour.

### VITAMIN E DEFICIENCY SYMPTOMS AND DISEASES
A combination of fatigue, loss of appetite, generalized soreness, and fever due to inflammation of body fat (steatitis or pansteatis).

### MY ADVICE FOR OWNERS
If you live in a city, it's important to include ample vitamin E in your cat's diet. Vitamin E works with vitamin A as an antioxidant, protecting your pet from the harmful effects of pollutants. These two vitamins, which potentiate each other, also maximize cellular membrane strength, keeping your cat's stored fat safe from oxidation, prepared to help ward off invasion by unwanted bacteria and viruses.

The best prevention against vitamin E deficiency is to keep your cat away from raw fish, cat foods with red tuna meat, and your own canned tuna fish. If your cat is a fish freak and refuses to change, mix some wheat germ (one half to one teaspoon) into your pet's daily meals. This can help counteract the possibility that the animal will develop steatitis.

Many commercial cat vitamin and mineral supplements contain insufficient amounts of vitamin E. If your cat is evidencing signs of steatitis (for example, yowls when you stroke its back, doesn't move around much), eliminate fish and fish-based food from the diet and get in touch with your veterinarian immediately.

## Vitamin K (Menadione)

### UNDERSTANDING WHAT IT IS
• A fat-soluble vitamin that a cat can form in the intestines.
• Necessary in forming the blood-clotting substance prothrombin.
• Can be depleted by X rays, radiation, mineral oil, and certain sulfa medicines used to treat urinary tract infections.
• It often appears on food labels as the additive phytonadione.

### How Vitamin K Can Benefit Your Cat

- Aids in preventing internal bleeding and hemorrhages.
- Promotes effective blood clotting.

### How Much Is Needed?

There is no recommended daily allowance, since cats manufacture their own vitamin K, which is normally sufficient.

### Best High-Quality Vitamin K Sources for Your Cat

Egg yolk (no uncooked white), yogurt, leafy green vegetables, alfalfa sprouts.

### Vitamin K Deficiency Symptoms and Diseases

Poor blood clotting (hypoprothrombinemia).

### My Advice for Owners

Cats rarely develop a vitamin K deficiency, except, perhaps, if they are being overdosed with mineral oil or are on an extended sulfa medication program. Yogurt or alfalfa sprouts added to your pet's diet are healthy, safe, and nutritious preventives.

Excessive bloody diarrhea could indicate an insufficiency of vitamin K, but this should be checked out immediately by your veterinarian.

If you are taking an anticoagulant medication such as Coumadin (warfarin), keep it out of an inquisitive cat's reach. Ingestion of warfarin (which is also in rat poisons) can dangerously deplete your pet of vitamin K and cause abnormal bleeding.

CAUTION: If your cat is being treated with heparin, an anticoagulant occasionally used in the treatment of DIC (disseminated intravascular coagulation), be aware that even natural foods containing vitamin K can reverse the drug's effect.

## Minerals

Without minerals, vitamins are virtually useless because they cannot be assimilated; and though cats can synthesize some vitamins in their bodies, they cannot manufacture a single mineral.

## *Calcium*

### UNDERSTANDING WHAT IT IS
• The mineral that, along with phosphorus, is most required in a cat's diet.
• It must exist in diet with approximately equal quantities of phosphorus (a calcium/phosphorus ratio of 1:1) to function properly and maintain strong teeth and bones and a healthy nervous system.
• For effective absorption and utilization, vitamin D must be present.

### HOW CALCIUM CAN BENEFIT YOUR CAT
• Promotes growth and maintenance of strong bones and teeth.
• Improves behavior by keeping nervous system functioning properly.
• Aids in blood clotting.

### HOW MUCH IS NEEDED?
The recommended minimum daily allowance is 200 to 400 mg for an average healthy cat. (More is required during pregnancy, lactation, and kitten growth periods.)

### BEST HIGH-QUALITY CALCIUM SOURCES FOR YOUR CAT
Milk and milk products, cheese, sardines, green vegetables.

### Calcium Deficiency Symptoms and Diseases

Decrease in bone density, limping, aversion to activity and movement, spontaneous fractures (osteoporosis). In nursing queens: trembling and rigidity (eclampsia). In kittens: swollen tender joints, arched back, and stiff legs (rickets).

### My Advice for Owners

Avoid feeding your cat an all-meat diet, and you'll avoid many problems. Meat-rich diets can cause a deficiency in calcium. Because meat has about fifteen times more phosphorus than calcium (organ meats, such as heart, liver, and kidney, have almost thirty to fifty times as much), the imbalance can cause your pet serious harm (see deficiency symptoms above).

Obviously, prevention is the best cure; but if it's too late for that, I'd suggest upping the calcium in your cat's diet. Supplements are available in several forms, so ask your vet about the right type and dosage for your pet. (If your cat likes ricotta cheese, one quarter cup will supply 167 mg of additional calcium.) Be patient. Deficiencies are not reversed overnight.

Don't attempt to overload your cat with calcium. This can result in other bone abnormalities, as well as decrease absorption—and cause possible deficiencies—of zinc, iron, iodine, and phosphorus.

It's important to remember that even though vitamin D is necessary for calcium absorption, an existing calcium deficiency or calcium/phosphorous imbalance can be worsened by adding more vitamin D to the diet.

## *Cobalt*

### Understanding What It Is

• Essentially a part of vitamin $B_{12}$ (cobalamin) that's needed for the manufacture of red blood cells.

### How Cobalt Can Benefit Your Cat
• Helps prevent anemia.

### How Much Is Needed?
The recommended minimum daily allowance is 0.16 to 0.2 mg for an average healthy cat.

### Best High-Quality Cobalt Sources for Your Cat
Meat, kidney, liver, milk, oysters, clams.

### Cobalt Deficiency Symptoms and Diseases
Same as for vitamin $B_{12}$.

### My Advice for Owners
Cobalt is only required when vitamin $B_{12}$ is deficient. Since strict vegetarians are the only group I know prone to $B_{12}$ deficiency, and I know no cats who are strict vegetarians, I feel confident in telling you not to worry about your pet's cobalt intake.

## Copper

### Understanding What It Is
• A mineral necessary for converting the iron in your cat's body into hemoglobin (the iron-containing pigment in red blood cells that carry oxygen from the lungs to the tissues).
• Important for the effective utilization of vitamin C.
• Often listed on food labels as the additive copper gluconate or cupric sulfate.

### How Copper Can Benefit Your Cat
• Increase energy and alertness by aiding effective iron absorption.

### How Much Is Needed?
The recommended minimum daily allowance is 0.02 mg for an average healthy cat.

### Best High-Quality Copper Sources for Your Cat
Beef, liver, peas.

### Copper Deficiency Symptoms and Diseases
Rare.

### My Advice for Owners
Relax. Your pet is getting adequate amounts of copper through meats and other animal products that are staples in cat diets.

## Iodine

### Understanding What It Is
- A particularly vital mineral for cats because it affects the function of the thyroid gland, which controls metabolism.
- Paradoxically, an undersupply can cause either hypothyroidism or hyperthyroidism (see deficiency symptoms below).
- It is contained in many prepared foods in the form of iodized salt.

### How Iodine Can Benefit Your Cat
- Promotes growth and altertness.
- Aids in weight control by burning up excess fat.
- Helps prevent and remedy both hypothyroidism and hyperthyroidism.

### How Much Is Needed?
The recommended minimum daily allowance is 0.01 to 0.02 mg for an average healthy cat.

### BEST HIGH-QUALITY IODINE SOURCES FOR YOUR CAT
Seafood (shrimp or scallops, for example), vegetables grown in iodine-rich soil.

### IODINE DEFICIENCY SYMPTOMS AND DISEASES
Lethargy, slow mental reaction, unexplainable weight gain (hypothyroidism), bulging eyeballs, nervous irritability, ravenous appetite, emaciation, enlarged thyroid gland (goiter or hyperthyroidism).

### MY ADVICE FOR OWNERS
Virtually all cat foods contain iodized salt, so the chance of your pet developing a specific iodine-related deficiency is rare. Other malfunctions of the thyroid gland can cause the conditions I've mentioned above and should be diagnosed and treated *only by a veterinarian.*

## Iron

### UNDERSTANDING WHAT IT IS
• Vital to forming red blood corpuscles (hemoglobin), which transport oxygen to the tissues.
• Important for the proper metabolization of B vitamins.
• Easily available and readily utilized from meat products as long as the cat has an adequate supply of copper, cobalt, manganese, and vitamin C.

### HOW IRON CAN BENEFIT YOUR CAT
• Improves the immune system and resistance to disease.
• Aids growth.
• Reduces absorption of lead and helps prevent its harmful effects.
• Cures or prevents an unlikely occurrence of iron-deficient anemia.

### How Much Is Needed?
The recommended minimum daily allowance is 5 mg for an average healthy cat.

### Best High-Quality Iron Sources for Your Cat
Liver, kidney, heart, farina, red meat, egg yolk (no uncooked white), asparagus, oatmeal, bran, lettuce, beets, tomatoes, cornmeal.

### Iron Deficiency Symptoms and Diseases
Impaired growth, lethargy (iron-deficient animals).

### My Advice for Owners
If you think feeding milk instead of cat food is spoiling your pet, you're underestimating the impact of your action: *You're ruining the animal's health!* Cow's milk contains only a very small amount of iron. And unless the milk is mixed with an iron-rich cereal, the nutritional benefits, especially as far as promoting growth and preventing anemia, are zero.

Iron supplements to a balanced diet are rarely needed.

## Magnesium
### Understanding What It Is
• A mineral important for the proper metabolism and usefulness of vitamins C, E, and B complex, calcium, phosphorus, sodium, and potassium.

• Used for converting blood sugar into energy.

• Essential for nerve and muscle functioning.

• The prime, oversupplied ash culprit in FUS (feline urologic syndrome).

• Often listen on food labels as magnesium phosphate or magnesium sulfate.

### How Magnesium Can Benefit Your Cat
• Helps in regulating body temperature and improving the cardiovascular system.
• Aids in modifying agitated behavior by working with calcium as a natural tranquilizer.

### How Much Is Needed?
The recommended minimum daily allowance is 4 to 8 mg for an average healthy cat.

### Best High-Quality Magnesium Sources for Your Cat
Shrimp, ground nuts, sardines, breast of chicken.

### Magnesium Deficiency Symptoms and Diseases
Rare.

### My Advice for Owners
Watch out for *oversupplying* your pet with magnesium. Most foods that cats eat supply much more magnesium than is needed, and it's the magnesium in ash (not ash alone) that primarily causes and aggravates FUS and other urinary ailments. (See chapter 11.) In fact, I recommend avoiding any dry food that contains more than 0.1 percent magnesium.

If your cat has urinary problems, do not use a daily multi-vitamin-mineral supplement without a vet's approval. Most of these contain at least seven or more milligrams of magnesium.

## Manganese

### Understanding What It Is
• An important mineral for good bone growth and structure.
• Necessary for a cat's proper utilization of biotin, vitamins $B_1$, C, and E, and fat metabolism.
• Aids in forming the principal hormone of the thyroid gland (thyroxin).

### How Manganese Can Benefit Your Cat
- Improves agility and alertness.
- Helps alleviate behavior problems by reducing nervousness.

### How Much Is Needed?
The recommended minimum daily allowance is 0.2 mg for an average healthy cat.

### Best High-Quality Manganese Sources for Your Cat
Egg yolk (no uncooked white), beets, whole-grain cereals, leafy green vegetables, peas.

### Manganese Deficiency Symptoms and Diseases
Rare.

### My Advice for Owners
Manganese is ample in most cat diets, so you don't have to fret about getting extra amounts into your pet's meals. Though this mineral is included in most commercial cat supplements, which advise one half to one tablet per day, the chance of any sort of toxicity is rare.

If you're feeding your cat a diet with very high amounts of calcium and phosphorus (see listings above and below), be aware that it could be inhibiting the absorption of manganese.

Note: Do not confuse manganese with magnesium.

## Phosphorus

### Understanding What It Is
- The mineral that works together with calcium and is therefore indispensable in your cat's diet.
- Should exist in a cat's diet with approximately equal quantities of calcium to function properly in maintaining strong bones and teeth and a healthy nervous system (vitamin D is also necessary for effective utilization).

TRIP TICKETS MONEY BOX

MAYROSA
Hand Made
...ARS

ONLY FOR

• Excessive amounts can result in calcium deficiency.
• It's found in many commercial foods, where it is listed as the additive calcium phosphate, sodium phosphate, or sodium pyrophosphate.
• It can be rendered ineffective by too much iron or magnesium.

### How Phosphorus Can Benefit Your Cat
• Increases energy by aiding in metabolization of fats and starches.
• Helps healing of bone and other injuries.
• Promotes healthier gums, teeth, and growth.

### How Much Is Needed?
The recommended minimum daily allowance is 150 to 400 mg for an average healthy cat.

### Best High-Quality Phosphorus Sources for Your Cat
Meat, egg yolk (no uncooked white), fish (cooked), whole grains.

### Phosphorus Deficiency Symptoms and Diseases
Rare.

### My Advice for Owners
Phosphorus is plentiful in animal protein, so deficiencies are rare. Unfortunately, excesses are not. It's important to always keep the calcium/phosphorus ratio in mind. It's calcium/phosphorus 1:1.

When you feed a balanced diet (see chapter 10), your cat will get all the pluses and none of the minuses of phosphorus. (Those minuses, by the way, can add up to problems if your pet is hooked on a single food with an inverse calcium/phosphorus ratio.) I feel strongly that all cats should be fed at least two different foods to prevent unhealthy addictions.

## *Potassium*

### UNDERSTANDING WHAT IT IS

• Working with sodium, this mineral regulates a cat's heart rhythms and water balance, enabling nerve impulses to be carried effectively to and from the brain.

• A nutrient that can be depleted by diarrhea, excessive sugar, diuretic medicines, and severe stress.

• On commercial foods it is often listed as one of the following additives: potassium chloride, potassium glycerophosphate, and potassium iodide.

### HOW POTASSIUM CAN BENEFIT YOUR CAT

• Helps in improving mental and muscular reflexes.

• Aids in allergy treatments and elimination of body wastes.

### HOW MUCH IS NEEDED?

The recommended minimum daily allowance is 50 to 100 mg for an average healthy cat.

### BEST HIGH-QUALITY POTASSIUM SOURCES FOR YOUR CAT

Beef, poultry, fish, cantaloupe, tomatoes, green leafy vegetables, bananas, cereals.

### POTASSIUM DEFICIENCY SYMPTOMS AND DISEASES

Rare, except in instances of excessive diarrhea or because of diuretic medication. (A protein deficiency would most likely develop first, causing lack of energy and muscle weakness.)

### MY ADVICE FOR OWNERS

Unless your cat is on some sort of diuretic medication (in which case, you should ask your veterinarian about what foods or supplements ought to be included in the animal's diet), or you're feeding kitty excessive amounts of sugary treats, don't worry about your pet's getting enough potassium.

If your cat has a kidney disease, potassium can accumulate

in the blood in toxic levels. Do not add any of the potassium-rich foods mentioned above to your pet's current meals, and definitely consult your vet about a special diet. Many serious problems can be averted if you tell your veterinarian what you're feeding your cat and ask if any of the ingredients are contraindicated because of the animal's condition. If you're using a commercial brand, bring in the label. Veterinarians want to help your pet as much as possible, but if you want their help, you have to help them by asking for it.

## Sodium Chloride

### UNDERSTANDING WHAT IT IS
• Works in conjuction with potassium in regulating fluid balance, muscle contraction, and nerve stimulation.
• Helps keep calcium and other vital minerals soluble (and therefore usable) in blood.
• In a word: salt!

### HOW SODIUM CHLORIDE CAN BENEFIT YOUR CAT
• Helps keep reflexes at optimal performance.
• Aids in preventing heat prostration.

### HOW MUCH IS NEEDED?
The recommended minimum daily allowance is 1,500 mg for an average healthy cat.

### BEST HIGH-QUALITY SODIUM CHLORIDE SOURCES FOR YOUR CAT
Salt (ample in all commercial cat food), shellfish, kidney, beets, bacon, grains.

### SODIUM CHLORIDE DEFICIENCY SYMPTOMS AND DISEASES
Possible weight and fur loss and dry skin. (Deficiency of sodium chloride is rare, except when heat or extreme exercise causes excessive loss of water and salt.)

## MY ADVICE TO OWNERS

Trust me on this one: Your cat is getting enough dietary sodium if you are feeding it any commercial brand of cat food.

Salt (not in excess, of course) is good for cats, because it makes them want to drink water—and water is essential, *particularly for dry-food eaters and older cats.*

## Zinc

### UNDERSTANDING WHAT IT IS

• A top-notch major mineral, necessary for protein synthesis, development of reproductive organs, contractibility of muscles, and tissue reconstruction.

• Destroyed by food processing.

• In commercial foods it is often listed as the additive zinc oxide or zinc sulfate.

### HOW ZINC CAN BENEFIT YOUR CAT

• Aids in healing wounds: burns, lacerations, flea bites, and skin abrasions.

• Helps in promoting growth and mental alertness.

• Aids in removing toxins from body and protecting against cancer.

### HOW MUCH IS NEEDED?

The recommended minimum daily allowance is 0.25 to 0.5 mg for an average healthy cat.

### BEST HIGH-QUALITY ZINC SOURCES FOR YOUR CAT

Lamb, pork, beef, egg yolk (no uncooked white), wheat germ, brewer's yeast.

### DEFICIENCY SYMPTOMS AND DISEASES

Retarded growth, weight loss, vomiting, conjunctivitis.

If your cat's diet is high in soy meal (check labels), more zinc is probably called for in the animal's diet.

It's good to remember that if you're adding zinc, your pet's need for vitamin A is increased. (Not drastically, because, if you recall, vitamin A is stored in a cat's body, and an oversupply can cause more harm than good. If you've forgotten, I'd suggest you reread the section on vitamin A and check with your vet before making any new dietary additions.) Zinc functions best when your cat is getting adequate amounts of calcium, phosphorus, and vitamin A.

## Water: The Nutrient You Never Think About

Let me state this briefly, succinctly, and emphatically: Cats need water. They can lose almost all of their body fat and protein and still survive; but if they lose more than one tenth of their body water, they can't. (Ironically, they are able to live without water longer than humans, but unrectified dehydration is inevitably fatal for both.)

In areas where there is hard water, cats get extra calcium and magnesium. If your pet has FUS, you might consider giving the animal bottled water that doesn't have a high magnesium content.

*Always keep fresh water available for your cat.*

## Questions and Answers About Nutrition ABC's for C-A-T-S

### VEGGIE VEXATION

*I'm sure my cat needs more roughage in his diet, because he's often constipated. But how can I get him to eat raw vegetables?*

I've found that grating and then marinating them in melted butter or chicken fat works best. Add just a pinch to his food to begin. *And I do mean just a pinch.* Too much will turn him off immediately. Once he begins accepting it, increase the amount (just slightly) each day until you find you can add from one to three tablespoons of grated greens, carrots, beets, sprouts (or boiled green beans, broccoli, or cauliflower) to his daily diet. Even better, add some brewer's yeast and bran mix to his meals. Also be sure he's eating a highly digestible food and getting ample liquids.

If the constipation continues, consult your vet. More than just a dietary deficiency might be the cause.

## ALLERGY DEFENSE

*When we take Mushka, our five-year-old male Siamese, with us to our country home in the summer, he sneezes, scratches, loses hair, and looks terrible. We don't let him outside and we feed him the same food we always do. Do you think this is a stress-psychological reaction or some sort of allergy? And what can we do about it?*

As prone to mood swings and unpredictable behavior as Siamese cats are, I suspect that Mushka is allergic to something (dust, mold, airborne spores) in your country home. I suggest supplementing his daily diet with 200 mg of vitamin C, a natural antihistamine, for at least a month or two before you plan to leave, and then continue the supplementation while you're there. (See chapter 11 for more about allergies.)

# Must-Knows
# for Mealtimes

✿❀✿❀✿❀✿❀

## The Wrong Way to Feed a Feline

*Don't feed your cat the way you would a dog—or a human being.*

Probably the biggest mistake people make about feeding is thinking that because both cats and dogs have paws and fur and often live as pets in the same household, their care and diet are the same. *Wrong!*

• Adult cats need almost five times more protein than do adult dogs.

• Cats require the amino acid taurine (which dogs do not) and *must* have it in their daily diet. (See "Protein" in chapter 2.)

• Cats need a daily intake of more B vitamins than dogs.

• *Dog food is nutritionally deficient for cats!*

A second mistake is the belief that what's good for people must be good or better for cats. *Wrong!*

• Canned tuna, which is fine for people, can kill a cat if fed as a daily diet.

• Cats have uniquely high nutritional needs for meeting their daily energy (kcal or calorie) requirements with quality, high-BV protein. (See chapter 2 for other "Differences That Make the Difference.")

## Counting Your Cat's Calories

*When filling your cat's calorie requirements, do it with calories that count nutritionally.*

It's extremely important to remember that quality protein—protein that is going to supply the proper amount of amino acids—is vital to your cat's health. A nutritious diet for an adult cat should contain a *minimum* of 30 percent of its calories from quality protein and a *minimum* of 20 to 40 percent from the right fats. (See chapter 2.)

| **Quick Converter** | 1 g protein | = 4 calories |
| | 1 g carbohydrate | = 4 calories |
| | 1 g fat | = 9 calories |

### Basic Calorie Needs for Cats

| Age | Daily Requirement per Pound of Body Weight | Approximate Amount Needed Daily |
|---|---|---|
| Newborn | 190 | 50 |
| 1–5 weeks | 125 | 125 |
| 5–10 weeks | 100 | 200 |
| 10–20 weeks | 65 | 290 |
| 20–30 weeks | 50 | 325 |
| Adult tom | 40 | 400 |
| Adult queen (pregnant) | 50 | 375 |
| Adult queen (lactating) | 125 | 690 |
| Adult male (neutered) | 40 | 360 |
| Adult female (spayed) | 40 | 220 |

There is a limit to how much—or how little—your cat will be satisfied with at mealtime. Therefore, you have to supply your pet with enough volume to satisfy the animal's internal stretch receptors (so that it feels full) and at the same time be sure that the volume you're feeding includes all the nutrients your cat needs. One cup of poor-quality food might fill your cat's tummy and supply ample calories but not even come close to meeting its nutritional requirements. (See chapter 4 for cat food comparisons).

## Mealtime Mistakes

*Understanding what they are and how to avoid them*

Cats are creatures of habit, and despite the press they've gotten in myth and fable, are very structure-oriented animals who flourish physically and emotionally on routine, particularly in matters of food and feeding. This type of behavior has its advantages and disadvantages for both owner and pet.

| ADVANTAGES | DISADVANTAGES |
|---|---|
| You decide what, where, when, and how much your cat will eat. | Your cat doesn't always agree with your decisions. |
| Your cat is secure in knowing where and when it will get its next meal. | Changes in schedule, feeding location, and especially food are not generally greeted with enthusiasm by your cat. |
| Being smarter than your cat, you can learn to avoid mealtime mistakes, plan ahead for food or schedule changes, keep your cat in optimal health, and make feeding trouble-free for life. | None. |

## *Most Common Feeding Mistakes*

### LEAVING FOOD AVAILABLE AT ALL TIMES

Cats are no more intrinsic nibblers than humans, and if you have an unlimited quantity of food lying about for either, it's going to be eaten—and eventually in excessive amounts. (See chapter 11 on obesity.)

If you're going to be away for the weekend, leaving dry food for your cat is fine, providing you've also arranged an ample supply of fresh water.

If because of personal or professional obligations you must allow your cat to self-feed, provide form and flavor variety right from the start. Cats, if permitted, will easily become addicted to one food to the exclusion of all others, which can be dangerous and even life-threatening, if a dietary change is deemed necessary in the event of illness.

Do not leave food available for nibbling if you intend to feed one or two balanced meals a day. Except for kittens and pregnant or lactating queens, cats do not need the additional calories of a round-the-clock buffet.

If you have a kitten and know you won't be home in time to serve the next meal until much later, wait until a few minutes after the kitten has eaten its normal meal and then place dry food into its dish. Don't worry if the kitten gobbles this down too; just refill the bowl. This is not going to be an everyday occurrence, so don't worry. The kitten will probably sleep a lot while you're gone and might not be overly hungry for the next meal, but you'll be assured that he or she will have enough food to eat even if you're delayed in returning.

Dry foods lose nutritional value when exposed to air.

Canned foods can spoil and cause gastrointestinal ailments if left out all day.

### FEEDING ONLY CANNED FOOD

Though canned meals (see chapter 4) have more protein and fat than dry or moist-packaged foods, you're paying more for palatability and water than for nutrition.

Cats fed only canned or moist-packaged foods are prone to tooth problems (accumulation of tartar), gum inflammation, bad breath, and other periodontal ailments.

### OVERSUPPLEMENTING WITH VITAMINS AND MINERALS

Whether they're in natural organ meats or professional vitamin supplements, oversupplementing your pet's diet can cause major health problems. Be particularly careful about vitamins A and D, calcium, and phosphorus. (Check the requirements and overdose cautions in chapter 2.) If you're feeding your cat a quality food, don't add any supplements that haven't been specifically prescribed. These can imbalance the food and counteract its nutritional effectiveness.

### FEEDING FROM THE SAME DISH

When cats get together, the dominant cat will get the larger portion of food (and nutrients). Even if Godzilla isn't hungry, competitive eating will inspire her to down more than half (if not all) of Peanuts' necessary portion. Keep their dishes separate, and in different locations if necessary.

### FEEDING FROM PLASTIC DISHES

A cat's nose is extremely sensitive, and because plastic is very porous it can retain odors, not all of which might be olfactory turn-ons for your pet. Your cat will turn away from its favorite food if the odor of an unpalatable previous meal is still present. Moreover, if the plastic has become scraped, bacteria can form in the ridges and cause gastrointestinal problems for your pet.

Hard ceramic or stainless-steel bowls and dishes are easier to keep clean and odor-free. But remember to *rinse well!* Sometimes even a change in dishwashing soap can cause a keen-nosed cat to spurn a favorite meal; in fact, a really repugnant odor can put a cat off food to the point of starvation. If you want to avoid washing and still maintain cleanliness, coated paper plates or Styrofoam bowls are fine to use, providing they're discarded after each meal and that you've secured them (either with a weight or double-stick tape) so your pet won't become frustrated by trying to dine on a too-easily-movable feast.

CAUTION: Do not wash your cat's feeding dishes with Lysol or strong bleaches. These substances can be toxic to cats, and if any remains on the dish, it could burn your pet's nose or tongue.

### FEEDING IN A NOISY OR ACTIVE ENVIRONMENT

Many cats are thought to be finicky eaters, or suffering from intestinal distress because of vomiting after eating, when in fact they are only reacting to their feeding location. Usually it's the kitchen and their food is put down for them at the same hectic time the family meal is being prepared.

Cats can lose their appetite when there is too much noise, too many people, or other pets in their environment.

### FEEDING YOUR CAT RAW MEAT

Yes, cats are carnivores, but just because they'll hunt outdoors and munch on an uncooked field mouse doesn't mean it's desirable for you to serve your pet raw meat. True, some nutrients are destroyed by cooking, but so are many destructive bacteria. (Salmonellae can grow quickly on meat and poultry that spend several days in a supermarket cooler before being purchased.) Believe me, it's worth the trade-off, especially where organ meats are concerned, since these are where roundworm larvae are usually found.

Unless you can buy fresh, flash-frozen meat (which is now available in some pet stores from Champion Foods as a product called Showbound), I advise cooking all meats until they are at least rare (or to a temperature of 140° to 165° F.). For owners who are intent on serving their cats raw meat: (1) Do not make it more than 25 percent of a complete or balanced diet; (2) be sure that meat is promptly refrigerated after it is purchased; (3) do not leave raw *or* cooked meat at room temperature for more than two or three hours; (4) *never feed raw poultry or raw fish.*

## FEEDING YOUR CAT LEFTOVERS

Table scraps can be added to a cat's regular meal provided they do not make up more than one quarter of the animal's daily ration.

*Never* feed your cat leftovers that you feel are unfit for human consumption.

## GIVING YOUR CAT HOMEMADE MEALS

If the diet is adequately formulated, homemade meals are fine for your pet. Unfortunately, as I've discovered in my treatment of sick cats, adequately formulated homemade meals are a rarity. Before you can say "Din-din is ready," your cat is going to decide what he or she does or doesn't like and become addicted to a particular food to the exclusion of others. That's when feeding and health problems begin.

You have to realize that what's nutritionally good for you is not necessarily adequate for your cat, and vice versa. If we ate the proportional amounts of protein and type of fat that cats need every day, we'd soon be in sad physical shape. On the other hand, there are additives in human foods that are safe for us but can cause major problems for cats.

If you feel you want to give your cat table food, limit the amount to one to three cups once a week. Make it a Sunday treat—it'll be fun for you and fine for your cat.

## PROVIDING TOO LITTLE WATER

If your cat eats dry food, leaving it a fresh supply of water every day is a necessity. An average seven-pound cat needs 200 ml (milliliters), or about six to seven ounces, of water daily. The water aids in metabolism of nutrients for energy, body temperature maintenance, and regulation fluid and electrolyte (ionized salts in blood, tissue fluids, and cells) balance. With dry food your pet is getting less than an ounce of water, which is insufficient for just about all of a cat's healthy bodily functions. (See the discussion of water in chapter 2.)

Even though many canned cat foods contain 75 percent

water, which would be an ample intake if this were a cat's sole diet (though not one I'd recommend), I'd still advise making fresh—or bottled (noncarbonated)—water available to your pet. Broth or tomato juice can substitute for fluid intake, but milk cannot. *Milk is a food and should not be considered a replacement for fluid.*

### MONO-FOOD FEEDING

Allowing your cat to eat only one food is setting your pet up for a fall from health. Though I've mentioned this before, it bears repeating: Cats are creatures of habit and can easily become addicted to a particular food to the exclusion of everything else.

Variety, for cats, is not only the spice of life—it's the key to it! No matter what "complete and balanced" food you are feeding your pet, I strongly advise feeding it another brand *at least* once (preferably two or three times) weekly. Different breeds and different environments, including a variety of stress conditions, create different nutritional needs that no one brand of cat food can cover.

Some brands will have more of certain minerals than others, for instance. By offering your cat minimal variety, you can cover all nutritional bases and provide maximum nutrition. In addition, accustoming your pet to various textures and tastes can prevent many problems (and trips to the vet) and often enable simple changes in diet to do the work of expensive medication—even surgery.

### THE WRONG TREATS FOR YOUR CAT

Bones—chicken bones, fish bones, sparerib bones, any bones that can splinter or break—can become wedged in your pet's mouth or stuck in its throat. (See chapter 7 for emergency treatments). Even though your cat may enjoy gnawing on a lamb or beef shank bone, it's still risky. Though the exercise might be great for your pet's gums, a large bone could break some teeth. In any event, after three to four hours without refrigeration, whatever meat is on the bone can develop bacteria, and the bone should be discarded. My advice is to avoid bones completely, and, instead, give your cat dry food for mealtime teeth-cleaning and gum exercise.

Milk is fine for young kittens, but many mature cats are unable to digest it because of a lactose intolerance and will develop diarrhea, which can cause dehydration.

Chocolate, though rich in arginine, an amino acid necessary for cats (see chapter 2), particularly in the prevention of ammonia intoxication, is high in the stimulant theobromine. Theobromine can diminish the flow of blood to the brain and, if ingested in excess, can cause heart attack. According to a recent study done at Newark's Beth Israel Medical Center, a six-ounce bar of chocolate could kill a five-pound cat. If you've allowed your cat to develop a liking for chocolate, you would be wise to keep it out of scent range and sealed tightly.

Raw egg white is not good for your cat. Despite all the movies you've seen where athletes add raw eggs to their breakfast drinks, the ativan in raw egg white can deplete your cat of vital biotin (see chapter 2) and undermine your pet's health. Egg yolk (the yellow part) is fine, and so is the white as long as the egg has been cooked.

Holiday cheer, especially in the form of rum-and-brandy-laced eggnog, should never be offered. Your cat might lap a small bit, become tipsy, and delight your guests. The amusement will be short-lived, however, if your pet develops a taste for alcohol (which is not uncommon) and takes to seeking it out whenever you have company or a drink. Alcohol can deplete your cat of all B complex vitamins as well as vitamin C, vitamin K, zinc, magnesium, and potassium, to say nothing of causing organ damage, hampering the liver's ability to process fat, and destroying brain cells. That's not what I'd call a treat.

## BAD TIMING

Giving your cat commercial kitty treats (such as Bonkers or Pounce) before meals (to put off having to feed your pet while you relax after coming home from work) or between meals (just as little snackies to show your affection) is a big mealtime mistake. These treats are manufactured to be highly palatable, and your cat will soon be clamoring for more than one—and chances are you'll soon be giving more than one. Not only will this diminish the cat's appetite, causing your pet to eat less of its regular food and therefore miss out on its nutrients that are required daily, but it can turn tabby tubby if not kept in check.

If you want to show love and affection to your cat, it's not necessary to do it with food. Blow bubbles and let your cat jump and break them. Jiggle a string around and watch your cat chase it. Crumple up a piece of wrapping paper and let your pet play solo soccer with it. *Feeding is a poor substitute for love. Play is a much healthier—and appreciated—alternative.*

Giving hair-ball medication before, with, or right after meals is quintessential bad timing. The medicine interferes with vitamin absorption and should be administered *between* meals! (See chapter 7 for the way to handle and prevent hair balls.)

## Culinary Curiosity Can Kill Your Cat

*If you believe that a cat would never eat anything harmful, there's a bridge in Brooklyn I'd like to sell to you.*

Hungry, bored, unsupervised, and, especially, very young cats will taste almost anything once—but once is all it takes for the occurrence of disastrous consequences.

The unwitting ingestion of toxic substances is one of the largest causes of feline fatalities.

As an owner (think parent), it's imperative that you be aware of substances in and around your home that can be potentially dangerous to your cat; that you take precautions to prevent your cat from gaining access to them; and that you know how to administer emergency remedies. (See chapter 7.)

*Possible Symptoms of Poisoning:* Excessive drooling, shaking and trembling of limbs, wailing or pained mewling, labored breathing, convulsions, vomiting, acute abdominal pain, lethargy, refusal to eat, diarrhea.

*Universal Antidote:* Symptoms of poisoning are very similar. If you are not sure what your cat has eaten and don't know the proper antidote, you can administer what is generally referred to as the universal antidote. The ingredients are easy to come by, and no cat owner should be without them.

> Combine 2 parts charcoal (which can be purchased at most pharmacies) or crumbled burned toast with 1 part milk of magnesia and 1 part tannic acid (or strong tea), or just use plain hydrogen peroxide. Feed 2–3 teaspoons to an adult cat and 1½ teaspoons to a kitten.

*Get your cat to the vet immediately! And take a sample of vomitus if possible.*

| HAZARDOUS SUBSTANCES (*Keep out of your cat's reach!*) | ADVICE |
| --- | --- |
| Antifreeze | Keep your cat from going under your car or into the garage. Many cats are attracted to the taste of antifreeze, but it can be lethal. Induce vomiting immediately (see chapter 7 for emetics and how to administer), give the universal antidote, remove any antifreeze on the cat's fur with mild soap and tepid water, wrap your cat in a towel, and rush to the nearest veterinarian. |

| HAZARDOUS SUBSTANCES (*Keep out of your cat's reach!*) | ADVICE |
| --- | --- |
| Household cleansers and detergents, all disinfectants (such as Lysol and pine oil), bleaches, oven cleaners, floor waxes, polishes (for silver or shoes, for example), toilet deodorizers, any sponges or rags that have been soaked with these products | Keep your pet out of the way when cleaning house. If any of these substances gets on the cat's paws or fur, wash it off with water and dry the cat. If your cat has swallowed any of these substances, check the bottle or can for the correct antidote. If none is available (or you don't know what's been swallowed), induce vomiting, give the universal antidote, and get your cat to a vet immediately. |
| Paints (particularly lead-based), water in old paint cans, artists' oils, turpentine, or any coal-tar product such as creosote, fuel oil, and gasoline) | Don't leave open paint cans where your cat can reach them. (A lid left in the yard can gather rainwater that your pet might sip.) Induce vomiting, give the universal antidote, and rush the cat to a vet. (If your pet brushes against a freshly painted surface, *never remove paint from fur with turpentine!* You can burn your cat's skin.) |
| All medicines, particularly boric acid, laxatives, aspirin, acetaminophen (Tylenol), tranquilizers, sedatives, and narcotics | Cat-proof your home and keep all medicines in closed containers. Something as seemingly harmless as boric acid can be fatal if eaten by your cat. Induce vomiting and immediately get in touch with your vet. |

Be wary, too, if your cat enjoys dining out occasionally on birds, mice, or other rodents. Pesticides, used to kill insects, can definitely be harmful to your pet, even when ingested secondhand. (If you spray to keep insects away, keep your cat away from insect eaters.) The toxins in your pet's al fresco meals can build up and cause slow but insidious poisoning. *Never use rodent poison in your home if your cat will be able to get at it or has a taste for mice!*

If you allow your cat outdoors, do not spray your lawn or trees with chemicals that can be toxic to cats. They'll lick their paws or eat the grass, and the unwanted chemicals can enter their system. You can find weed-killing sprays that are non-toxic to animals at your local nursery.

There are dozens and dozens of substances (far too numerous to mention individually) in and around your home that are harmful to cats. My simple safety rule is this: *If it's something you think could harm a child, keep it out of your cat's mouth.*

## Owner Precautions for Plant Eaters

*If your cat's a plant eater, be sure your plants are safe to eat!*

Greens and grasses are sought instinctively by cats for a variety of reasons, but if their selection is limited by environment, they don't always make the right choices, and protecting them from the wrong ones is up to you.

*The Whys and the Wise:* Domestic cats usually seek out greens to cleanse their intestines (either of hair balls or foods they wish they hadn't eaten). They do so because of an innate desire for plant matter (which in an undomesticated feline is obtained from the stomach of its prey), a dietary lack of vitamins (particularly vitamin C and the B complex), or—in the case of some house cats—simply out of boredom or to demonstrate their anger at something you've done . . . or haven't done.

Whatever the reason, supplying your cat with safe, nibbleable greens is a wise idea. Eliminating dangerous ones is even wiser.

## THE GOODIES

**Alfalfa sprouts**

Great nutrient source and easy to grow indoors.

**Catnip** (*Nepeta cataria*)

Some cats enjoy it as a zesty, energizing treat; others seem to get happily high on it. They sniff it, lick it, chew it, rub themselves against it, and roll around in it. The live plants do not seem to cause the often frenzied behavior that the dried leaves do, and most cats prefer the growing plant to the dried leaves when there is a choice. In fact, they'll usually eat the entire plant. Kittens under three months old tend to ignore catnip, and Siamese cats, as a general rule, are not impressed by it. Then again, it takes a lot to impress a Siamese.

**Parsley**

Can be grown indoors or in a garden. Fine for cats—and you, too.

**Rye or wheat grass**

This can be planted easily in your garden or obtained from pet stores and grown in an apartment window-box.

**Thyme**

Cats enjoy sniffing and nibbling this herb, though it offers none of the stimulant excitement of catnip or valerian. In fact, it often causes quite the opposite reaction, leaving the cat pleasantly laid back and content.

**Valerian** (*Valeriana officinalis*)

Cats respond to this the way they do to catnip. Interestingly, both valerian and catnip, though outwardly stimulating to cats, are used in internal tranquilizing preparations.

## THE BADDIES

**Bittersweet**

The orange berries are pretty but can be deadly if eaten.

**Christmas (pine) trees**

Keep your pet away from the water stand under the tree. If your cat decides to take a drink, the animal might ingest some pine needles. These contain pine tar, which aside from preventing absorption of vital nutrients can cause serious gastrointestinal problems.

**Dieffenbachia**

If you don't know what types of plants are in your home, it's your responsibility as a cat owner to find out. Dieffenbachia, also known as dumb cane and the mother-in-law plant (because if a piece of the stem is put on the tongue or chewed, it can render a person speechless for a short time), has a fast-acting toxicity for cats. It causes labored breathing, severe mouth irritation, and intense abdominal cramps very quickly after ingestion. If this happens, induce vomiting immediately (see chapter 7) and rush your pet to a veterinarian for an antidote.

**Jerusalem cherry (Christmas cherry)**

This small bushlike houseplant stays enticingly pretty for weeks with bright red or orange berries, which are highly toxic if ingested and can cause cyanide poisoning.

**Laurel (sheep laurel or mountain laurel)**

Frequently used in floral arrangements, laurel can poison your pet. If you have any in your home and notice some missing, watch your cat for symptoms such as discharge from eyes and nose, excessive salivation, vomiting, and limb trembling or paralysis. Call your veterinarian quickly if such symptoms are present.

**Philodendron and other large-leaf ivies**

These common houseplants are frequently nibbled on by cats, and the effects of repeated ingestion are cumulative. It may take one to three months for symptoms of poisoning (see above) to appear.

**Poinsettias**

Holiday beauties in any home but dangerous for greens-seeking cats. The leaves can cause skin, eye, mouth, and stomach inflammations.

**Other leaves your cat should leave alone:**

| | |
|---|---|
| Arrowgrass | Locoweed |
| Azalea | Mistletoe |
| Hemlock | Oleander |
| Jimsonweed | Peach leaves |
| Larkspur | Rhubarb leaves |
| Lily of the valley | Wisteria |

## New-Life Preventive Nutrition Tactics

*A fortified immune system can help your cat fight back.*

When a cat's diet is imbalanced or inadequate, so is the animal's immune system—the defense force your pet depends on for warding off illness, protecting against toxins, healing injuries, mobilizing energy, and preserving good health. Since you're in charge of your pet's diet, the strength of that defense force depends on you!

*Preventive Ammunition:* Today's cats are exposed to more toxic substances than ever before, which is why they need more high-powered immune-building nutrients in their diet.

Adding extra vitamins C and E to your cat's daily fare is a simple and smart dietary safeguard. (See chapter 2 for best sources and ways to administer.)

If your cat is in good health and eating a high-quality food regularly (see chapter 4) or is currently on my New-Life Diet (see chapter 10), an *additional* supplement of 100 mg of vitamin C, 50 mg of vitamin B complex, and 10 IU of vitamin E daily is an optional but advisable immune-system booster.

On the other hand, if your pet is neither in top shape nor eating quality food regularly, I'd suggest these supplementary programs:

For adult cats
   Vitamin B complex, 50–75 mg daily
   Vitamin C, 200–400 mg daily
   Vitamin E, 10–15 IU daily

For aging cats
  Vitamin B complex, 50–100 mg daily
  Vitamin C, 250–500 mg daily
  Vitamin E, 15–30 IU daily (five days a week)
  (Can be divided in two doses each day with meals)

For pregnant or lactating cats
  Vitamin B complex, 75–100 mg daily
  Vitamin C, 300–500 mg daily
  Vitamin E, 15–30 IU daily
  (Can be divided in two or three doses each day with meals)

For kittens (over three months)
  Vitamin B complex, 50 mg daily
  Vitamin C, 150–250 mg daily
  (Can be divided in three doses each day with meals; do not give pills; see chapter 5 on kittens)

## Questions and Answers
## About Must-Knows for Mealtimes

### CALORIE CONFUSION

*I'm a new (and conscientious) cat owner, but I just don't understand the difference between calories, kilocalories, and kcals. I'd like to be sure my cat is getting his proper daily caloric intake, but I don't know how many calories are in a kcal. Is there a simple conversion formula?*

Very simple. None. For your purposes (and the purpose of this book), a calorie is a kilocalorie and a kcal. Whether your cat needs 40 calories, kilocalories, or kcals per pound of body weight daily, if he weighs eight pounds, he's going to need 240 of any one (or all) of them.

What's important to remember is that the calories in a cup of dry food and a cup of canned food—or a cup of leftovers—are not the same.

## MUCH ADO ABOUT MUSHROOMS

*I've just learned that mushrooms can poison cats and I'm a total wreck. A few months ago, Randikins, my three-year-old Burmese, took to eating those left over from my salad. He seemed to like them, so I began adding more just so that he could enjoy the leftovers. Now I'm terrified. He looks okay, but could poison be accumulating in his system?*

If you're okay, Randikins is okay. The onset of mushroom poisoning is usually quite rapid and caused by ingestion of toxic wild mushrooms (particularly *Amanita muscaria* and *Amanita phalloides*). A cat who has eaten a toxic wild mushroom or toadstool will evidence obvious symptoms of poisoning (excessive salivation, vomiting, tremors, paralysis). Since Randikins has acquired a taste for mushrooms, I'd suggest you don't let him out in an area where he can find any on his own. (If he ever does, and you suspect poisoning, induce vomiting immediately and rush him to your vet.) As long as you keep buying your mushrooms at the produce market, relax and enjoy those salads with your pet.

## SLOPPY EATER

*I always thought cats were neat and clean, but my two-year-old mixed breed tiger-striped cat, Sheena, can't eat a meal without splattering food on the wall or floor. Oh, she'll lick herself clean afterward, but I'm left with washing the baseboard and mopping up the floor. Is she being hostile, or what? And is there anything I can do about it?*

You could start by putting her food in a deeper feeding dish, and then placing that dish away from the wall on newspaper, or switch her to a dry food. I doubt if she's being hostile. It sounds as if she's really hungry and gobbling down her food quickly. Maybe if you fed her earlier—or more often—she'd slow down.

## LIVING WITH A LEAF LOVER

*My cat snacks on my houseplant leaves as if they were after-dinner mints. I give her a pet vitamin daily, so I can't believe she has a nutritional deficiency. She also gets lots of love and attention. Have you any idea why she does this? And any suggestions for saving my plants?*

I can think of numerous reasons why your cat might be a leaf nibbler, but *you* will have to zero in on the right one. She might need more nondigestible (cellulose) fiber in her diet (such as beet pulp or bran) to cleanse her intestines. Try giving her a salad once in a while (see chapter 10 for recipe suggestions) and see what happens.

On the other hand, her attraction for your plants might be nothing more than the motion of the leaves (from a breeze, fan, or whatever), which excites her hunting instinct.

As for saving your plants, you can buy cat repellent sprays at pet stores, which might help. Other than that, all I can suggest is to hang your plants from the ceiling and hope for the best.

## NO CAN DO

*Is it all right for me to feed my cat food directly from the can?*

I don't recommend it. There's no harmful substance in the can (such as lead), but after you open it with a can opener there might be jagged edges around the top that could injure your pet's mouth or tongue. And because the can is light, your cat will have difficulty eating, most likely spending its mealtime pushing and chasing its dinner around the room.

## DISHING IT OUT

*I was told that I shouldn't leave my cat's water bowl right next to his food dish. Why not?*

Because cats use their tongues to get food into their mouths—and don't always do so neatly—so food remnants can easily drop into the water, spoil, and contaminate it. That is the reason I'm not in favor of those double feeding dishes with one side for water and the other for food. A little distance between the food and water dishes is all that's necessary, and don't forget to keep the water fresh.

# PART TWO

# *Feeding the Right Stuff*

# *Let's Talk Cat Food*

✿✿✿✿✿✿✿✿

## Cat Food Categories Simplified

*What makes the difference*

In the vast kingdom of pet foods there are two basic categories:
supermarket/commercial food and alternative/professional
food. Since they are often misunderstood, and I refer to them
frequently throughout the book, it's important that you understand their differences.

### *Supermarket/Commercial Food*

Available across the nation in supermarkets and grocery
stores, advertised extensively and expensively on TV and in
magazines, these pet foods pander to *people* and, in most cases,
offer more hype than nutrition. Ingredients may vary in
quality from shipment to shipment—even from can to can—
depending on the ups and downs of the commodities market.

In fact, a particular brand of chicken dinner that you buy for your cat on one day might have different ingredients when you buy it again on another. And I'm talking about *name* brands!

Store-label pet foods often have even wider ingredient-quality fluctuations, and generics are the nutritional pits. In a recent study 85 percent of generic brands tested failed to meet minimum NRC (National Research Council) levels for one or more essential nutrients, and more than 50 percent failed to meet their own label guarantees!

### Alternative/Professional Food

Available only in pet shops, feed stores, health food stores, or from breeders and veterinarians, these foods do not advertise on TV or in mass-market publications. They don't have to. Their advertisements are, have always been, and will continue to be results: healthier animals! Visibly healthier animals. These foods are made and formulated to offer cats the best possible nutrition. Breeders and veterinarians have always known this, but often fail to impress upon owners the definite benefits their pets can reap—and the myriad problems that can be avoided—by simply feeding them quality ingredients in fixed formulas.

Though great nutritional strides have been made recently by national, name-brand pet food companies, I still feel that alternative foods, in general, can provide superior feline health fare.

## The Four Cat Food Types Explained

*Know your options for optimal cat health.*

There are four types of food for cats: canned, semimoist, dry, and homemade. (I'm excluding such occasional feline fast foods as birds, mice, moles, and so on, since I consider these random and circumstantial choices that only cats—and not their owners—can make.)

Understanding what these foods are, their nutritional and economic advantages and disadvantages, and deciding what they offer your cat in the way of health and you in the way of convenience are essential for the successful revitalization and lifetime fitness of your pet.

## Canned Food

**Advantages**
• High in fat; more palatable than dry food.
• Contains more digestible meat proteins than dry food.
• Has a high caloric density, which means your cat can easily meet daily energy requirements.
• Food is cooked in the can, destroying potential disease-causing bacteria.
• Has a longer shelf life than dry or semimoist food.
• Has less chance of insect or bacterial infestation than other types of food.
• Doesn't necessarily need preservatives.

**Disadvantages**
• High moisture content, which means you're paying a lot of money for water. For cats with FUS this is an advantage, since increased liquid intake is recommended.
• Food-processing heat causes loss of nutrients.
• Many brands contain color additives (for aesthetic appeal to owners), some which could be carcinogenic (cancer-causing). All have the potential to adversely affect a cat's physical and emotional health.
• Many manufacturers disguise TVP (textured vegetable protein) so that it looks like animal protein.
• Improper storage (extended exposure to heat or cold), which often happens in large supermarkets, can destroy nutrients and palatability.
• Needs refrigeration after opening.

## Semimoist Food

**Advantages**
- Comes in convenient, easy-to-serve pouches or cans.
- Doesn't spoil if left out the way canned food would.
- Because of processing techniques, this type can contain more added nutrients than canned food, but not as many as dry food.
- Quite palatable, but not as palatable as moist canned food.
- Has a higher caloric density than canned or dry food, but only because of its sugar content, which comes primarily from propylene glycol. This is a binder used to prevent bacteria and fungi formation, as well as to retain moisture, and is useful in the control of diarrhea.

**Disadvantages**
- Contains a variety of artificial colorings, some of which could be carcinogenic (cancer-causing), all of which could adversely affect a cat's physical and emotional well-being.
- The propylene glycol used as a binder is a sugar and can increase the risk that a cat will develop diabetes.
- Costs more than equivalent cat foods.
- High in salt and magnesium.

## Dry Food

**Advantages**
- Low in moisture with a high concentration of nutrients.
- Cheaper than canned food.
- Doesn't require refrigeration; easily stored.
- Can be left in the cat's feeding dish all day without spoiling.
- Can promote dental health by decreasing tartar accumulation.
- Has a high content of nondigestible fiber, which has been

shown to be effective in decreasing the incidence of colon cancer and lowering blood sugar.

• Generally has a better vitamin-mineral assay than canned food, because of the lower water content.

**Disadvantages**

• Must have preservatives, many of which can pose health risks for allergy-prone cats.

• Highly vulnerable to pathogens (microorganisms or substances, such as molds, insects, and fungi, which are capable of causing disease).

• Frequently lower in fat and therefore less palatable than canned food.

• Higher in cereal content and difficult for many cats to digest.

• Any nutrient to which a cat could react adversely may be ten times more concentrated in dry form. On the other hand, any nutrient to which a cat responds favorably could be ten times more effective.

• With the exception of some alternative brands, mineral content is often too high, particularly in salt and magnesium.

• Owners tend to leave food out all day for free feeding, which can create a finicky eater and cause obesity. I am totally against free feeding unless you have a kitten in need of food when you can't be there, have a sick cat, or are going away and have no one to feed your pet.

• Some dry foods absorb moisture from the stomach and can expand, leading to blockages in the intestines.

## *Homemade*

### Frozen Purchasable Homemade

These are professional, flash-frozen, uncooked pet foods that are sold only in pet stores, health food stores, feed stores, and by some veterinarians for owners who want to cook their cats' meals themselves. They are available in two forms:

1. A complete and balanced meal that supplies total nutrition and requires only a stove or microwave and an owner's personal touch. (Total Feline by Showbound, from Champion Foods, is the most widely available in this form.)

**Advantages**
- Owner doesn't have to worry about balancing nutrients.
- Ingredients are fresher and haven't been overly processed.

**Disadvantages**
- More expensive than other types of cat food.
- Less convenient and more time-consuming to feed.

2. Single-protein ingredients, such as chicken, liver, beef, and fish, which owners can use to prepare whatever recipes they feel their cats would enjoy. (These are available from numerous companies, including Showbound, Jespy, Northern Plateau, and Abady.)

**Advantages**
- Meat, poultry, and fish for pets is less expensive than that for people.
- Owners can tailor recipes to their pets' individual needs.

**Disadvantages**
- Recipes are often imbalanced and deficient in necessary nutrients.

### Owner Homemade

These are meals made from an owner's recipes with the owner's selection of ingredients.

**Advantages**
- Ingredients are readily available and protein is usually of higher BV quality with fewer artificial-flavor additives.
- Recipes can be tailored to a cat's individual needs.

**Disadvantages**
• Recipes are frequently imbalanced and deficient in necessary nutrients.
• Additives that are GRAS (generally recognized as safe) for humans can be harmful to cats.
• More time-consuming than feeding prepared cat food.

## Table Scraps

These are meals made solely from the leftovers of family meals, usually all meat.

**Advantages**
• Inexpensive and convenient.

**Disadvantages**
• Meals are imbalanced, deficient in adequate nutrients, frequently all meat, and generally detrimental to a cat's health.

### What to Look for on a Cat Food Label

*Getting the most for your cat and your money*

## 1. A National Brand Manufacturer

The label should say "Manufactured by . . ." and give the manufacturer's address. If the label says "Distributed by . . ." or "Manufactured for . . .," the food is usually of inferior nutritional quality. (Unfortunately, low-priced food generally means low-quality nutrition.) *For your cat's sake, check it out.* Write to the manufacturer and ask the following questions:

*What is the protein utilization of your food?*
Even though the ingredients might be there, you want to know if the food was processed correctly, whether ample vitamins and minerals were included for adequate utilization of

those ingredients, and whether the named nutrient percentages are what your pet is actually getting. Think of it this way: Even a meat loaf with prime ingredients can be cooked to nutritional destruction.

*What is the total protein digestibility of your food?*
You want to know if the protein sources, which might be identical to those listed in other brands, are of better quality and therefore offer a higher digestibility.

*What is the caloric density of your food?*
You should know how many calories there are in a can, a cup, or a pound, so that you can adjust your pet's meals accordingly.

*What are the names and credentials of your plant's staff?*
You want to be sure there is a process engineer, a biochemist or qualified technician supervising the production of this food.

*Do you have in-house testing? Or where is your product tested?*
You want to know that all the ingredients have been tested for purity and quality—before and after processing—and that they have the facilities to do such testing.

## 2. Nutritional Guarantee

The label should state that the food is "complete," "adequate," or "balanced," and guaranteed to meet or exceed all NRC requirements for growth and maintenance of adult cats and growing kittens. If the label states that the evidence is based on feeding trials made in accordance with AAFCO (American Association of Feed Control Officials) standards, this is even better. (See "How to Examine Cat Food for Quality" below.)

## 3. Guaranteed Analysis

The percentages of nutrients in the food are usually listed above, below, or next to the ingredients on cat food labels. Protein and fat are usually given in minimum amounts, since they are the most expensive ingredients. But a large minimum guarantee of protein does not mean that the product's protein is going to be of high-BV quality. Algae, coconut, cottonseed, wheat, soybean meals, and others are classified as "plant proteins," which can boost the protein percentages on labels without providing equivalent nutrient benefits—especially for cats, who require *animal* protein.

A close ratio of fat to protein is your best indicator of the usable protein your pet is getting. For example: A canned food with a crude protein minimum of 10 percent and a crude fat minimum of 7 percent is a better choice than one with a crude protein minimum of 13 percent and a crude fat minimum of 4 percent.

Keep in mind that without a substantial amount of fat, the food's calorie content will be so low that excessive amounts will have to be eaten just to meet the cat's daily energy requirements.

## Quick Guide to Healthy Buys

### Dry Food
- Minimum protein should be 30 to 35 percent.
- Minimum fat should be at least 15 percent.
- Maximum ash should be no more than 8 percent.*
- Maximum moisture should not be more than 12 percent.

*A "low ash" content does not mean that the food is necessarily low in magnesium, which is a contributing factor in FUS. Magnesium content should not exceed 0.10 percent.

**Canned Food**
- Minimum protein should be 10 to 12 percent.
- Minimum fat should be at least 3 percent.
- Maximum ash should be no more than 3 percent.*
- Maximum moisture should not be more than 77 percent (simply because you'll be paying more for water than nutrition).

**Soft-Moist Food**
- Minimum protein should be 24 percent.
- Minimum fat should be 8.5 percent.
- Maximum moisture should not be more than 34 percent.
- Ash content should not exceed 7 percent.*

## 4. Ingredients

Each ingredient in a pet food must be listed on the product label in descending order by weight to provide a general indication of the product's content and quality.

The first four ingredients listed should contain at least two sources of high-BV protein (such as meat, fish, poultry, or cheese).

In the entire ingredient panel there should be:
- no more than two digestible carbohydrates
- some source of animal fat (if not specifically listed and the protein/fat ratio is close, a sufficient amount is usually present)
- no more than one preservative
- a long list of vitamins and minerals (the longer the better)
- no artificial coloring

(See "Understanding Ingredients" below.)

---

*A "low ash" content does not mean that the food is necessarily low in magnesium, which is a contributing factor in FUS. Magnesium content should not exceed 0.10 percent.

And my personal advice is to avoid any cat foods containing:

**Gluten meal**
The residue from processed wheat, corn, and other carbohydrates. Can cause a malabsorption of food from the intestinal tract (gluten enteropathy) and a variety of intestinal problems.
**Whey**
The liquid left after the curd and cream are separated from milk. Can cause intestinal problems in cats with a lactose intolerance.
**Barley hulls**
The outer covering of barley. A poor form of fiber, offers zero nutrition, and can cause many feline intestinal problems.
**Wheat shorts**
The residue of wheat processing and milling. A poor supply of fiber that can adversely affect cats allergic to gluten and can cause intestinal problems as well as nutritional deficiencies.

## Understanding Ingredients

*You don't have to pronounce them, but you should know what they are if your cat is eating them.*

Because of man-made feed components and labeling technicalities, looking at cat food ingredients and trying to figure out which ones are proteins and which ones are carbohydrates, which are vitamins and which are additives, is not easy. Since this knowledge is essential to evaluating a food as well as potentiating your pet's health, the following category breakdown of ingredients should simplify things.

## *Most Common Cat Food Ingredients*

### High-BV Protein Sources

Meat (flesh from beef, pork, goat, lamb, mutton; may
include skeletal muscle, flesh from tongue, esophagus,
diaphragm, and heart)

| | |
|---|---|
| Beef | Whole egg |
| Liver | Poultry giblets |
| Kidney | Poultry by-products |
| Ocean whitefish | Liver meal |
| Tuna | Chicken |
| Beef by-products | Meat by-products |
| Fish meal | Meat meal |
| | Poultry by-products meal |

### Backup Protein Sources to Boost Protein Content

| | |
|---|---|
| Fish solubles | Textured soy protein (TVP) |
| Hydrolized poultry feathers | Soy flour |
| Digest (liquefied, chemically predigested meat) | Whey |
| Soybean meal | |

### Amino Acids (Essential Components of Protein)

| | |
|---|---|
| L-Lysine | MHA |
| DL-Methionine | |

### Fat Sources

| | |
|---|---|
| Chicken fat | Soybean oil |
| Wheat germ oil | Cod-liver oil |
| Animal fat | Safflower oil |
| Fish oil | |

### Carbohydrates (Digestible)

| | |
|---|---|
| Brewer's rice | Ground yellow corn |
| Rice flour | Wheat flour |
| Corn gluten meal | Wheat germ meal |
| Cornmeal | Ground corn |

## Preservatives and Additives
Sodium nitrite (preservative and color fixative; may be carcinogenic)
Sodium nitrate (may be carcinogenic)
MSG (monosodium glutamate; a concentrated source of sodium)
BHA (butylated hydroxyanisole; an antioxidant used with fat to keep it from becoming rancid)
BHT (butylated hydroxytoluene; excess can adversely affect kidneys)
Ethoxyquin (chemical preservative)
Propylene glycol (sugar)
Caramel coloring (artificial coloring; an additive)
Guar gum (a binder; plant carbohydrate)
Guaiac gum (chemical preservative)
Vegetable gums (binders; plant carbohydrates)
Benzoic acid (chemical preservative)
Propyl gallate (chemical preservative; may be a cause of liver damage)
Citric acid (chemical preservative)
Ascorbic acid (chemical preservative; also vitamin C)
Titanium dioxide (a natural food coloring)

## Carbohydrates (Nondigestible, Fiber)
Beet pulp
Rice hulls
Cellulose

## Vitamins
Brewer's yeast (excellent source of multiple B vitamins)
Pyridoxine/Pyridoxine hydrochloride (vitamin $B_6$)
Vitamin A acetate/Vitamin A palmitate (vitamin A)
Menhaden meal (dried fish extract and an excellent source of vitamin $B_{12}$)
Choline/Choline chloride (member of the B complex)
Inositol (member of the B complex)

a-Tocopherol/DL-alpha tocopherol acetate (source of
   vitamin E; an antioxidant)
Thiamine/Thiamine mononitrate (vitamin $B_1$)
Riboflavin (vitamin $B_2$)
Ascorbic acid (vitamin C; also classified as a preservative)
Folic acid (member of the B complex)
Niacin/Niacinamide/Nicotinamide (vitamin $B_3$)
D-activated animal sterol (source of vitamin $D_3$)
Biotin (member of the B complex)
Menadione/Menadione sodium bisulfite complex (source of
   vitamin K)
Cyanocobalamin concentrate (source of vitamin $B_{12}$)
Calcium D-pantothenate/d-Calcium pantothenate (vitamin
   $B_{15}$)
Para-aminobenzoic acid (member of the B complex)
Lecithin (formed by combination of choline and inositol)


**Mineral Sources**
Calcium carbonate/Calcium iodate (calcium)
Sodium/Sodium tripolyphosphate (salt)
Ferrous sulfate (iron)
Potassium chloride (potassium)
Manganese sulfate (manganese)
Manganous oxide (manganese)
Zinc oxide (zinc)
Iron carbonate/Iron sulfate (iron)
Copper oxide (copper)
Cobalt carbonate (cobalt)
Ethylene diamine dihydroiodide (iodine)
EDDI (iodine)
Bonemeal (phosphorus and calcium)
Sodium selenite (selenium)
Phosphoric acid (phosphorus with fluorine)
Defluorinated phosphate (phosphorus with low fluorine)
Sorbic acid (chemical preservative)
Potassium sorbate (chemical preservative, similar to fat)

## How to Examine Cat Food for Quality

*Look before you feed.*

### The Home Test for Dry Food

• Fill a glass with water and drop a piece of dry food in it. As it dissolves, watch what comes out. You don't want to see a lot of chicken feathers or hair.

• Check for *consistency* of size, shape, and density of pellets. They should be uniform. Each piece contains a certain amount of nutrients, and if some of the pieces crush to powder between your fingers while others remain rock hard or vary in size, the manufacturer's extruding equipment (which makes the pellets) is poor, and the product is not likely to be any better.

• Beware of dry food bags that feel greasy on the outside. If the fat has soaked through, the food has been left susceptible to rodent, insect, and bacteria infestation.

• See if the food contains a large amount of "fines" (tiny crumblike particles). A little in any dry food is to be expected; a lot means that the food is not of high quality.

• Smell the food. It should not have a peculiar, moldy, or rancid odor.

• Examine the food for *color consistency*. Any greenish, bluish, blackish, or pale pellets in an otherwise color-consistent batch could indicate mold.

• Check the bag's contents for any foreign material, such as rodent waste, paper, and insects. Be particularly careful about insects. Many owners feel, oh, it's just another source of protein; but some insects have tiny porcupinelike barbs that can damage a cat's esophagus. Take my advice and don't bother to put the insect under a microscope—get the bag of food out of your house.

• Dry food has a shelf life of six months. Once opened, it should be stored in a sealed container and kept no longer than one month.

### The Home Test for Canned Food

• Be sure that there is no swelling or raised bump on the can. Both usually indicate that the vacuum in processing has been broken, and the product can be harboring disease-causing bacteria.

• For a large can, open both ends and push the food onto a platter (or use three small plates). Cut the food into thirds (top, middle, bottom) and compare the three sections. All three sections should have a homogeneous consistency: Equal distributions of fat and other ingredients should be evident.

• For small cans, or those with stewlike consistency, put the food on a plate and examine it. You don't want to see pieces of large blood vessels, tendons, or ligaments. (These are not high-BV protein meat by-products.) You also don't want to see a large glob of fat in the middle. Fat should be well distributed throughout. In small cans fat sometimes rises to the top; this is all right. It's the big glob of poor-quality fat that you want to avoid. There should be no hair, feathers, or any other foreign material in the food.

• Refrigerate the unused portion of canned food, but do not keep it longer than two days.

### The Home Test for Soft-Moist Food

• Be sure that the package is tightly sealed. A small tear leaves contents an easy target for contamination.

• Soft-moist pellets should be uniformly soft. When crumbled between your fingers, you should not feel crunchy hulls or crackly, fibrous substances.

## How Do Name Brands Stack Up?

*My name-brand breakdown to help you select the food that's best for your cat's health*

The brands I've included in this section are among those most widely distributed and purchased in the United States. Individual flavor varieties listed in each category are not all-inclusive, but I feel that they provide ample representation of a particular product line as marketed at the time of this writing. I've limited my comments to those flavor varieties that differ in some respect from the others when I felt that this difference could be of significant importance to the health of your cat. Where I have made no entries, the general comments for the product apply. In all instances, these comments are neither intended, nor should they be construed, as either endorsement or condemnation of any product or manufacturer.

## *9 Lives Cat Food*

*9 Lives, Amore, 9 Lives Crunchy Meals, Tender Meals*

Star-Kist Foods, Inc.
582 Tuna Street
Terminal Island, CA 90731

### CANNED FOOD

*General Comments:* All varieties of 9 Lives canned cat food meet or exceed the NRC recommendations for growth of kittens and maintenance of adult cats, and have identical amounts of vitamins as well as zinc, manganese, iodine, copper, and selenium, all of which are above NRC requirements.

| NAME | MY COMMENTS |
|---|---|
| Beef & Liver Platter | Low magnesium |
| Chicken & Cheese Dinner | Low magnesium |
| Chicken Dinner | Low magnesium |
| | |
| Choice Cuts 'n' Cheese | |
| Chopped Platter | Good protein/fat ratio, slightly higher in iron than others; poor sodium/potassium ratio, which can adversely affect nerve and muscle function in debilitated cats |

| NAME | MY COMMENTS |
|---|---|
| Country Chicken 'n' Gravy | Low magnesium |
| Fish & Liver Feast | Slightly higher in magnesium |
| Fisherman's Stew | |
| Kidney Entrée | Low Magnesium |
| Kidney in Creamed Gravy | |
| Liver & Bacon | Good protein/fat ratio; slightly higher in iron than others; poor sodium/potassium ratio, which can adversely affect nerve and muscle function in debilitated cats |
| Liver & Chicken Dinner | Low magnesium |
| Liver & Egg in Creamed Gravy | |
| Liver in Creamed Gravy | |
| Mackerel Dinner | Slightly higher in magnesium |
| Ranch Supper | Low magnesium |
| Savory Stew | |
| Scrambled Egg & Beef | |
| Seafood Platter | Slightly higher in magnesium |
| Sliced Beef | |
| Sliced Turkey | |
| Sliced Veal | |
| Super Supper | Slightly higher in magnesium |
| Tuna & Chicken | Slightly higher in magnesium |
| Tuna & Egg | Slightly higher in magnesium |
| Tuna & Liver | Slightly higher in magnesium |
| Tuna in Sauce | Slightly higher in magnesium |
| Western Menu | Good protein/fat ratio; slightly higher in iron than others; poor sodium/potassium ratio, which can adversely affect nerve and muscle function in debilitated cats |

| NAME | MY COMMENTS |
|------|-------------|

### *Amore*

| NAME | MY COMMENTS |
|------|-------------|
| Braised Liver | Varieties come in three-ounce |
| Chicken Heart & Liver | cans. All flavors listed here |
| Home Style Dinner | contain gluten meal and |
| Ocean White Fish & Tuna | whey, which I have found to |
| Poached Salmon | cause chronic diarrhea and |
| Sea Food Supper | other intestinal problems in |
| Simmered Beef Dinner | many cats. |
| Turkey & Giblets Dinner | |

### DRY FOOD

*General Comments:* The three varieties of 9 Lives Crunchy Meals currently available (Real Liver & Chicken, Real Tuna & Egg, and Super Supper) all meet or exceed the NRC recommendations for growth of kittens and maintenance of adult cats.

### SOFT-MOIST FOOD

*General Comments:* All varieties of 9 Lives Tender Meals are complete and balanced according to NRC recommendations for growth of kittens and maintenance of adult cats. Unfortunately, all varieties contain artificial coloring, more than one preservative, and corn gluten meal, which may be the cause of chronic diarrhea in some cats.

Adult cats (six to eight pounds) need one three-ounce pounch of 9 Lives Tender Meals daily, which equals one cup of dry cat food. Dividing the amount into two half-cup (one-and-a-half-ounce) servings is recommended. Providing fresh water at all times is essential.

| NAME | MY COMMENTS |
|------|-------------|
| Salmon, Shrimp & Cheese | All contain essentially the |
| Supper Supper | same basic ingredients; di- |
| Tuna & Egg | gest (liquefied, chemically |
| | predigested meat) is sprayed |
| | on to justify different flavors |
| | and is not a great source of |

| NAME | MY COMMENTS |
|------|-------------|
| | quality protein. The ratio of protein to fat is poor, and I do not like the high sugar and salt content of the food, particularly for mature cats (these can be bad for the heart and could cause diabetes), or the artificial colorings in it. |

## Purina Cat Food

*Purina Variety Menu, Catviar, Tender Vittles, Happy Cat, Whisker Lickins, Thrive, Kitten Chow, Cat Chow, Meow Mix, Alley Cat, Special Dinners*

Ralston Purina Company
St. Louis, MO 63164

### CANNED FOOD

*General Comments:* Purina manufactures more than twenty varieties of canned cat food. Though all are not listed here, all are complete and balanced to meet or exceed the NRC nutrition recommendations for growth and maintenance of kittens and cats. Varieties mentioned here, unless otherwise noted, all contain sodium nitrite (a possible carcinogen).

| NAME | MY COMMENTS |
|------|-------------|
| Beef & Liver Dinner | |
| Chicken Dinner | No sodium nitrite; chicken is first ingredient. |
| Country Dinner | |
| Hearty Stew | |
| Kidney Dinner | |
| Liver Dinner | No sodium nitrite |

| NAME | MY COMMENTS |
|------|-------------|
| Tender Beef Dinner | |
| Tuna | |
| Tuna & Chicken Dinner | |
| Tuna & Egg Dinner | |

## *Catviar* (tab-opening cans)

| | |
|------|-------------|
| Beef & Liver Entree | All contain sodium nitrite |
| Poultry Entree | (a possible carcinogen) and |
| Rainbow Trout Entree | ethoxyquin. |
| Salmon & Crab Entree | |
| Seafood Entree | |

## DRY FOOD

*General Comments:* All varieties of Purina dry food meet or exceed NRC nutritional recommendations for growth and maintenance. All listed here, except where noted, contain artificial coloring, no animal protein source in the first four ingredients, and contain gluten meal and whey.

| NAME | MY COMMENTS |
|------|-------------|
| Alley Cat (Poultry & Seafood flavor) | |
| Cat Chow (Country Blend, Original Blend) | |
| Kitten Chow | No artificial color; has animal protein in first four ingredients. |
| Meow Mix (Tuna, Liver & Chicken) | |
| Special Dinners (Dairy Dinner, Farm Style Dinner, Sea Nip Dinner) | |
| Thrive (The Four Food Groups Cat Food) | |

### SOFT-MOIST

*General Comments:* All varieties of Purina's "moist" meals are complete and balanced to meet NRC recommendations for all life stages. Unfortunately, all contain artificial color, more than one preservative, and corn gluten meal, which may cause chronic diarrhea in some cats.

| NAME | MY COMMENTS |
|---|---|
| Happy Cat (Moist & Meaty, Seafood & Beef) | None of these soft-moist varieties lists the necessary |
| Tender Vittles (Beef, Gourmet Dinner, Hearty Platter, Liver, Seafood, Tuna) | two sources of high-BV protein within the first four ingredients. |

## Carnation Cat Food

*Fancy Feast, Tidbits, Buffet, Bright Eyes, Friskies, Fish Ahoy, Chef's Blend*

Carnation Company
Los Angeles, CA 90036

### CANNED FOOD

*General Comments:* All varieties of Carnation canned cat food meet or exceed the minimum nutritional levels established by the NRC for kitten growth and adult cat maintenance.

| NAME | MY COMMENTS |
|---|---|

### *Fancy Feast*

| | |
|---|---|
| Beef and Chicken Feast | All varieties listed (except |
| Beef and Liver Feast* | where noted) are low in mag- |
| Chopped Grill Feast | nesium, but contain sodium |
| Country Beef Feast | nitrite and a poor protein/fat |

*Higher in magnesium than others.

| NAME | MY COMMENTS |
|---|---|
| Country Chicken Feast<br>Fancy Seafood Feast*<br>Ocean White Fish & Tuna<br>Savory Salmon Feast<br>Tender Liver & Chicken<br>  Feast<br>Turkey & Giblets Feast | ratio. An average cat would need to eat three of these small cans to meet daily nutritional needs. |

### Tidbits

| | |
|---|---|
| Beef & Cheese in Sauce<br>Cape Cod Style Platter<br>Country Style for Cats<br>Poultry & Cheese in Sauce<br>Poultry Bits in Sauce<br>Prime Bits in Sauce<br>Seafood Bits in Sauce | All varieties listed here (except Beef & Cheese in Sauce) are low in magnesium, do not contain sodium nitrite, but are high in carbohydrates. |

### Friskies Buffet

| | |
|---|---|
| Country Style<br>Liver & Chicken<br>Mixed Grill<br>Prime Entree<br>Salmon Dinner<br>Tuna Dinner<br>Turkey & Chicken Entree<br>Turkey & Giblets | All varieties listed here (except Tuna Dinner) are low in magnesium. |

### Bright Eyes

| | |
|---|---|
| Beef & Liver Dinner<br>Deluxe Entree<br>Liver & Chicken Dinner<br>Seafood Dinner | All varieties listed here contain sodium nitrite. An average cat must eat nine ounces of these meals to meet daily nutritional requirements. |

*Higher in magnesium than others.

## DRY FOOD

*General Comments:* All varieties of Carnation dry cat food meet or exceed the NRC recommendations for growth of kittens and maintenance of adult cats. All varieties listed have a poor protein/fat ratio and more than one preservative.

| NAME | MY COMMENTS |
|------|-------------|
| Chef's Blend | |
| Fish Ahoy | Contains artificial color |
| Friskies (Braised Liver Flavor, Country Chicken Flavor, Gourmet Flavor, Ocean Fish Flavor) | |
| Little Friskies | |

## *Kal Kan Cat Food*

*Kal Kan, Crave*

Kal Kan Foods, Inc.
Vernon, CA 90058

## CANNED FOOD

*General Comments:* All varieties of Kal Kan provide complete and balanced nutrition for all stages of a cat's life, as substantiated by AAFCO (Association of American Feed Control Officials) established testing procedures, meet or exceed NRC requirements, and contain approximately thirty-four calories per ounce. All canned varieties contain more biotin and choline than other supermarket/commercial brands.

| NAME | MY COMMENTS |
|------|-------------|
| Beef & Heart Dinner | |
| Bits o' Beef Dinner | |
| Country Chicken Dinner | |
| Kitty Stew | |

| NAME | MY COMMENTS |
|------|-------------|
| Mealtime for Finicky Eaters | |
| Moist & Tender Bits | Lower in magnesium than others |
| Poultry Dinner | Lower in magnesium than others |
| Salmon Supreme Dinner | |
| Simmered Supper | |
| Sole & Cod | |
| Tender Turkey Dinner | |
| Tuna | |
| Tuna & Chicken Platter | |

## DRY FOOD

*General Comments:* Provides complete and balanced nutrition for all stages of a cat's life, as substantiated by AAFCO (Association of American Feed Control Officials) established testing procedures and meets or exceeds NRC requirements. One eight-ounce cup provides 353 calories.

| NAME | MY COMMENTS |
|------|-------------|
| Crave | Contains artificial coloring, but not more than one preservative; nutritionally above most supermarket/commercial dry foods. |

## Alternative/Professional Brands

## Science Diet

*Feline Maintenance, Feline Growth*

Mill's Pet Products, Inc.
P.O. Box 148
Topeka, KS 66601

### CANNED FOOD

*General Comments:* Science Diet canned cat food is 100 percent nutritionally complete and balanced, professionally formulated for optimum nutrient intake and utilization, and available only in fifteen-ounce cans from feed stores, pet stores, health food stores, and veterinarians. It comes in two formulations: Feline Maintenance, for adult, nonreproducing cats; and Feline Growth, for kittens and pregnant or lactating queens.

| NAME | MY COMMENTS |
|---|---|
| Feline Maintenance | High in quality animal fat and low in magnesium, important factors in the prevention of FUS; protein of good biological value; food digestibility excellent, which is evidenced by fewer, firmer, and less odorous stools. |
| Feline Growth | Vitamins and minerals are effectively increased and balanced to maximize utilization of higher fat and protein content needed during growth and reproduction. |

### DRY FOOD

*General Comments:* Feline Maintenance and Feline Growth are as complete, balanced, and scientifically formulated for their respective purposes in dry form as they are in canned.

| NAMED | MY COMMENTS |
|---|---|
| Feline Maintenance | Low magnesium; the high caloric density gives the cat more energy with less food. |
| Feline Growth | Same as for canned food. |

## Iams Cat Food

> The Iams Company
> Lewisburg, OH 45338

### Dry Food Only

*General Comments:* Iams is guaranteed nutritionally complete and balanced for all stages of a cat's life and meets or exceeds the requirements for growth as established by the NRC. Top high-BV protein, quality animal fat, maximum vitamins and minerals scientifically formulated for optimum food digestibility and utilization, and a low magnesium content for prevention of FUS. One of the oldest established alternative-food manufacturers, Iams is known for quality and dependable quality control. I've seen just a quarter cup of Iams fed twice daily, along with fresh water, turn a thoroughly dilapidated seven-year-old stray into a sleek, spirited feline that was definitely "the cat's meow."

## Cornucopia Natural Cat Food

*Super Stars*

> Veterinary Nutritional Associates, Ltd.
> 229 Wall Street
> Huntington, NY 11743

### Canned Food

*General Comments:* The three varieties of Cornucopia canned cat food currently available (Super Stars, Super Stars Beef & Liver, and Poultry Dinner) exceed the NRC requirements for all life stages. All use levels of megavitamins and chelated minerals, are relatively low in magnesium, and do not contain added artificial preservatives, colorings, flavorings, sweeteners, or sugars. Cans are available in six-and-a-half-ounce as well as fifteen-ounce sizes.

### Dry Food

*General Comments:* Super Stars is Cornucopia's only dry cat food at present. It exceeds the NRC requirements for all life stages, and, like Cornucopia's canned varieties, has a relatively low magnesium content, uses megavitamins and chelated minerals, and contains no added artificial preservatives, colorings, flavorings, sweeteners, or sugars.

## Triumph Cat Food

*Triumph Low Ash, Hi-Tor*

Triumph Pet Industries
P.O. Box 100
Hillburne, NY 10931

### Canned Food

*General Comments:* Triumph's canned cat food currently comes in ten Low Ash varieties: Beef, Liver, Chicken, Beef & Liver, Beef & Chicken, Beef & Heart, Beef & Kidney, Beef & Cheese, Beef & Egg, Beef Liver & Bacon. These meet the nutritional requirements for all life stages, as substantiated by feeding studies performed under AAFCO testing procedures, and are available in six-and-a-half-ounce as well as fourteen-ounce sizes.

### Dry Food

*General and Personal Comments:* Hi-Tor All Natural Cat Food is Triumph's dry cat food. It is nutritionally complete and balanced for all stages of a cat's life, meets or exceeds the nutritional requirements for growth and maintenance as established by the NRC, and is low in ash, phosphorus, and magnesium. This is fine, but I don't think it is right for an "all natural" cat food to advertise as such, when the additive "ethoxyquin" is clearly printed on the ingredient panel. Also, "wheat shorts" (a poor source of fiber that can adversely affect cats allergic to gluten) is the second ingredient, and the only protein in the first four ingredients is the last: poultry by-product meal.

## Tamiami Cat Food

> Beatrice Companies, Inc., Specialty Pet Products
> P.O. Box 58
> Nashville, TN 37202

### CANNED FOOD

*General Comments:* Tamiami canned cat food meets or exceeds nutritional requirements as established by the NRC for growth and maintenance of adult cats and growing kittens. It has a fine protein/fat ratio, is low in magnesium, has no artificial colors or additives, and among the first four ingredients are three high-BV-protein sources. It comes in fourteen-ounce cans and is one of the best economical-nutrition buys on the alternative cat market.

### DRY FOOD

*General Comments:* Tamiami dry cat food, like its canned counterpart, meets or exceeds nutritional requirements as established by the NRC for growth and maintenance of adult cats and growing kittens. It also has a fine protein/fat ratio and is low in magnesium.

## Questions and Answers About Let's Talk Cat Food

### REGAINING DIETARY BALANCE

*When I found Podie as a kitten two years ago, I fed her whatever brand of food was on sale and never thought anything about it. But when her vet bills began getting out of hand (because of constant colds, skin irritations, eye infections, you name it) I realized I had to think about it and began giving her lots of vitamins and miner-*

*als. They seemed to help at first, but now she's become listless, her appetite is erratic, and she looks terrible. Does she need other supplements, or could I be giving her too many already?*

Overdosage is a possibility, but I couldn't say for certain, since I don't know what or how much you've been giving. What I do know, though, is that it is very common for a nutritionally deficient diet to become even worse if incorrectly supplemented. I've discovered that in almost all cases, dietary imbalances cause more problems than do insufficiencies, which sounds to me to be what's happened to Podie.

My advice is that you stop attempting to improve inadequate foods and start feeding professionally formulated, complete, and balanced ones. For Podie I'd recommend Feline Maintenance (Hill's), Iams (Iams), Lick Your Chops (Lick Your Chops), or Showbound's Total Feline (Champion Pet Foods), which can be obtained at most pet, feed, and health food stores, or from veterinarians. Hold off on all supplements unless they've been specifically prescribed and your vet knows exactly what your Podie is now eating. Be sure she is getting fresh water daily and that her food dish is kept clean. She should show a marked improvement within ten to twelve days. If not, veterinary attention is needed.

## COMPLETE TREAT MISUNDERSTANDING

*I know Pounce is supposed to be a treat food, but it's labeled 100 percent nutritionally complete for growth and maintenance, and my eleven-year-old Siamese (an ultra-finicky, picky eater) loves it. Would it be all right to feed it to him as a regular diet?*

As far as I'm concerned, it not only wouldn't be all right, it would be all wrong. Take a look at the ingredient panel. There are *more* than three preservatives. There is artificial coloring, sugar your Siamese's pancreas doesn't need to deal with at his age, a poor protein/fat ratio, and certainly more carbohydrates (count 'em) than I'd want any cat to ingest at mealtime on a regular basis. The Quaker Oats Company's Puss 'n Boots Pounce treats are meant to be snacks and should be fed only as such. (See chapter 3.) Their money-back guarantee is—and rightly so—for "satisfaction," not for nutrition.

## PROFESSIONAL DIFFERENCE

*I know that all professional foods are alternative foods, but does that mean all alternative foods are indeed "professional"?*

I'm glad you asked, but unhappy to have to answer no. Professional food manufacturers can back the optimum nutritional value and specific dietary purposes of their products with over thirty years of extensive, documented research, as well as animal feeding and performance tests. Additionally, professional foods are quality-controlled and coded, so that in the event spoilage occurs because of improper storage during shipment, or whatever, that particular batch can be recalled. This is not true of all alternative foods, many of which have been formulated only on paper, do not have the same substantial research and track-record credentials, and therefore do not meet the criteria of a "professional" food.

## UNGUARANTEED GUARANTEES

*I've always bought my cat's food with the highest minimum protein percentage on their guarantee. But I recently met a breeder who told me that these guarantees are about as nutritionally valuable as the paper they're printed on. How can pet companies get away with this?*

In some instances your friend might be right. Gross analysis of protein can mean very little. (The leather in four pairs of old shoes could well give a crude protein guarantee of 10 percent.) It is, for instance, not uncommon for the labels on generic pet foods (or those from small pet food companies who only intend to keep their products on the market long enough to make quick money) to misrepresent their contents. But, as a rule, the pet industry is well regulated by the FDA, local and state agencies, and the U.S. Department of Agriculture. Misrepresentation on labels is highly unlikely among name-brand or reputable alternative food manufacturers.

## HEALTHIER HEALTH FOODS?

*Are there "health foods" for cats? If so, what are they, and are they really better than other foods?*

There are many foods whose makers claim they are "health foods," but I've found them to be, in effect, nothing more than alternative foods with ingredients (such as garlic or herbs) included—or excluded—more to impress people than to improve cat nutrition. As far as I'm concerned, when a product does not contain two sources of high-BV animal protein in the first four ingredients, it's not a "health food" for cats.

# Feeding for Fitness

❖❀❖❀❖❀❖❀

## Know Your Cat's Age

*Knowing the human equivalent of your cat's age will give you a better understanding of your pet's nutritional needs.*

When does a kitten become a cat? A lot sooner than most owners realize. Technically, kittens are kittens until they're a year old, but a female enters puberty somewhere between three and nine months of age and can come into heat as early as three and a half months! Males are a little slower. They become pubescent around the age of seven months.

Being aware that your eight-month-old kitten is the feline equivalent of a thirteen-year-old teenager makes the cat's high nutritional requirements a lot more comprehensible. Everyone realizes that a growing, active teenager needs more daily protein, fat, vitamins, and minerals than the average forty-year-old office worker, and food quantity and supplements are adjusted accordingly. But everyone does *not* realize that this also holds true for cats. A six-year-old cat that's still being fed the same diet and quantity as an eight-month-old kitten is going to be one plump puss with mounting pounds of health problems. (See "The Dangers of Feline Obesity" in chapter 11.)

Also, as a cat ages, its sense of smell and taste decrease, often causing an older animal to refuse its usual food. Weight loss and accompanying nutrient depletion at this stage of a cat's life can be extremely dangerous to its health. Knowing what highly palatable digestible foods and supplements are called for is essential (see "New-Life for Your Beloved Older Cat" later in this chapter), as is knowing your cat's age.

The following comparisons are given to help guide you in providing appropriate and optimum nutrition throughout your pet's life. (All ages are in years, except where indicated.)

| Cat's Age | Human Age Equivalents |
| --- | --- |
| 6 months | 10 |
| 8 months | 13 |
| 1 | 15 |
| 2 | 24 |
| 4 | 32 |
| 6 | 40 |
| 8 | 48 |
| 10 | 56 |
| 12 | 64 |
| 14 | 72 |
| 16 | 80 |
| 18 | 88 |
| 20 | 96 |
| 21 | 100 |
| 22 | 104 |

## Prime Meals for Pregnant Cats

*Feed your queen like a queen and the results will be royally rewarding.*

Taking care of kittens before they are born is more your job than the mother's. Professional breeders have known for years that the better nutritional and physical shape a queen (pregnant cat) is in, the healthier her litter will be. An overweight cat who becomes pregnant, for instance, is a high risk for delivery complications, including kitten deformities and fatalities.

Considering that your pet is going to be pregnant for only a little more than two months (sixty-three to sixty-six days is the average gestation period), paying extra attention to her diet for that short a time is a minor inconvenience that will pay both of you back with major rewards.

No doubt about it, a pregnant cat must be provided with a constant supply of necessary nutrients for the proper fetal development of her kittens. In fact, a recent study at Colorado State University proved conclusively that a queen's diet directly affects the growth and health of all her kittens' vital organs.

## Nutrient Musts for Moms-to-Be

*Vitamins A and D:* If insufficiently supplied, growing fetuses will draw minerals from the mother and could cause serious nutritional deficiency in the queen.

*Vitamin B complex:* Needed for prevention of birth defects and protecting the queen against debilitating effects of stress.

*Vitamin C:* Important for reducing pregnancy stress and strengthening the queen's immune system.

*Calcium and phosphorus:* Vital for protecting the queen from mineral deficiency and for enabling the production of nutritive milk; necessary for proper growth of kittens' bones and teeth and preventing malformations.

*Copper, iodine, and zinc:* Inadequate amounts in diet can cause birth defects in kittens.

## *Meals Fit for a Queen*

A pregnant cat should be fed two, or preferably three, times daily. Dividing her daily ration into three portions is easier on the digestive system and will make her more comfortable during this period.

During the first month of pregnancy, her protein intake should be increased, but not her calorie intake. If you are not feeding a quality food, replacing one fourth of her regular meals with cooked—not raw—liver, chicken, beef, fish, kidney, or any high-BV protein will supply needed nourishment without excess calories. Extra fat is stored in muscle tissue, and since the uterus is composed of this tissue, you want to keep it lean and firm. Good muscle tone is important for an easy and safe delivery.

During the second month of pregnancy, caloric needs are greater. Where a cat would ordinarily need forty calories per pound of body weight daily, when pregnant she needs at least fifty. I'd advise increasing your mommy-to-be's *daily* food intake by 25 to 75 percent, depending on her size and appetite. Add additional food to each of her meals; don't give it all at once. Her abdomen doesn't need an onslaught of extra pressure. Again, provide the increase in the form of high-quality protein food (chopped cooked liver, egg yolk, chopped cooked white meat turkey or chicken, salmon, cheese), making sure that her mainstay diet is complete and balanced.

Special commercial diets are available for pregnant and lactating cats. These can be obtained from veterinarians and pet food stores and are well worth the extra cost.

During this stressful period, an abundance of tender loving care and a little special mealtime catering now and then will be greatly appreciated by your pet—and can make you both feel terrific. The following are New-Life recipes formulated as healthy, occasional *treat* meals for pregnant cats. Lactating and nursing queens require more food (depending on their size and the size of the litter, they can eat three to four times as

much as they did before pregnancy), so these recipes should be doubled for them.

## SPECIAL BREAKFAST

¼ cup cooked white meat turkey or chicken, chopped
¼ teaspoon brewer's yeast
1 teaspoon soybean oil
1 teaspoon finely grated mild Cheddar cheese

Mix all ingredients. If cat prefers a more moist texture, add a tablespoon of warm chicken broth.

## LUNCHEON TREAT

⅛ teaspoon brewer's yeast
1 tablespoon tomato juice
2 sardines, chopped
2–3 cooked chicken livers, chopped

Mix brewer's yeast with tomato juice and pour over sardines and liver. If cat doesn't like tomato juice, substitute evaporated milk or broth.

## DINNER DELIGHT

¼ teaspoon wheat germ
¾ teaspoon soybean oil
1 egg yolk (not white), beaten
¼ teaspoon brewer's yeast
¼ teaspoon butter, melted
1 tablespoon ricotta or cottage cheese
3 ounces drained canned salmon or 4 ounces quality canned food

Mix wheat germ, soybean oil, egg yolk, brewer's yeast, and butter, then add ricotta or cottage cheese. Stir well and fold into the salmon or quality canned food.

### HEALTHY SNACKS

• Cantaloupe balls, two or three daily. They're low in calories and high in vitamin C and B vitamins.

• One or two tablespoons of yogurt. It's a good source of calcium and vitamin K.

• Cooked (fresh or canned) asparagus spears. Cats enjoy playing with and nibbling on them, and they supply iron.

• Small pieces of tomato. Tomato supplies potassium, vitamin C, and selenium, which helps vitamin E work more effectively.

• One or two small squares of mild cheese. A great source of calcium and protein.

• A couple of canned or raw peas. A fine source of vitamin A and fun for cats to bat around.

• Leftover cooked vegetables, eggs, meats, and broth can be mixed into regular balanced meals, but should not amount to more than 25 percent of the cat's usual serving.

### No-No Snacks

• Spicy luncheon meats
• Italian sausage or pepperoni
• Chili
• Chocolate, spinach, or rhubarb. They contain oxalic acid, which can interfere with the proper absorption of needed calcium.
• Grains and cereals. These contain phytic acid, which can impair calcium absorption.
• Extremely fatty foods (such as greasy table scraps, tallow, lard) can cause digestive upsets and impair calcium absorption.

### Pregnancy Cautions

• *Do* make sure your cat has a booster distemper vaccination before pregnancy.

• *Don't* overfeed your cat with meals or treats. In the last week or two of pregnancy, be particularly careful. This is when she needs the most protein, vitamins, and minerals, and the least amount of pound-adding carbohydrates.

• *Do* allow your cat normal exercise, but if she is used to outdoor athletics, such as jumping from tree branches or window ledges, I'd suggest grounding her once she's into her second month of pregnancy.

• *Do* give your cat supplemental vitamin C if she's not getting at least 200 to 400 mg daily.

• *Don't* supplement your pet's diet with multiple-vitamin-mineral preparations without consulting your veterinarian. *Supplementing an inadequate or imbalanced diet incorrectly can cause even more harmful imbalances. For optimal health, there is no substitute for a balanced and adequate diet.*

• *Do* use only highly digestible foods (such as egg yolks, cooked meats, cottage cheese, and salmon) to increase caloric intake when supplementing meals of pregnant—and especially nursing—queens.

• *Don't* give your cat commercial worm medicine while she's pregnant. Consult your veterinarian for a safe treatment.

• *Do* avoid low-quality or generic dry foods, which often cause digestive upsets (diarrhea or vomiting) in pregnant queens and nursing cats, who have voracious appetites.

## Getting Kitty Started

*Picking up nutritionally where Momma leaves off can keep your kitten fit for life.*

There's nothing like a mother's milk, particularly colostrum (the first milk produced after birth) to give a kitten the best possible health start in life. Colostrum contains the queen's antibodies, along with quality nutrients, which are passed on to the kittens in the first three days of nursing, providing them with an immediate immune system to fight off the wide variety of possible kittenhood infections and diseases.

A healthy queen will produce ample milk for her kittens for four or five weeks. After that the quantity of milk usually decreases and the kittens should be weaned, gradually.

*Smooth Transition:* When weaning a kitten, make the switch pleasant, nutritional, and digestibly rewarding. (You wouldn't expect a baby to go directly from breast to Big Mac, so don't expect a kitten to go from Mom's milk to Meow Mix without a howl.) An intermediate stage called "mush" is what I've found to be most successful on all levels.

## Mush Menus

### STARTERS

Anytime after three and a half weeks, you can mix a little bit of Pablum with warm skim milk (or Borden's KMR, or Hill's Feline p/d mixed with water) and offer it to the kittens on your finger. The sooner they learn how to lap (instead of suck), the easier the transition to feeding from Mom to meal bowl will be.

### DR. JANE'S TWO-TO-ONE KITTY SLURPIES

Blend a half cup canned complete and nutritionally balanced cat food with a quarter cup skim milk, water, or Borden's KMR. The consistency should be about that of junior baby food. Once your kitten accepts the mush, decrease the amount of liquid daily. Around the age of six weeks, your kitten should be ready and eager for solid meals—canned or dry. If you prefer to get your kitten used to dry food, blend two parts dry food with one part skim milk (or water, Borden's KMR, evaporated skim milk, or whole milk if it doesn't cause loose stools). Again, slowly decrease the amount of liquid in the mush. But always keep fresh water available in a *shallow* bowl! *Don't* use Fido's deep water dish. A kitten could tumble in and drown.

### ALTERNATIVE BEGINNINGS FOR ORPHAN KITTENS

Use any professional weaning formula (such as Borden's KMR), which can be obtained from your veterinarian or pet food store; or my home recipe:

Equal parts evaporated whole or skim milk mixed with
  boiled water
1 egg yolk
1 teaspoon Karo or maple syrup per pint mixture
1 teaspoon brewer's yeast or bee pollen per pint mixture
A vitamin-mineral supplement (such as Fauve or Vital Nutrition)

Mix well and keep refrigerated until needed. Warm before
feeding. Temperature should be tepid.

Orphan formulas can be fed from baby-doll bottles, special
bottles available from vets or pet stores, or plastic medicine
droppers. *Never feed a kitten on its back!* Place the animal on its
stomach on a towel on your lap. Open the kitten's mouth
gently and then insert the dropper or nipple. Be sure the
nipple opening is not clogged! Keep it at an angle that will
allow milk to flow slowly, yet prevent air from being sucked in.
Pulling back occasionally on the bottle or dropper will stimulate the kitten's sucking reflex. Burp after feeding just as you
would a baby. The kitten's tummy should feel full but not
bloated. Four feedings a day are often sufficient, but I prefer
five—and find that most kittens do, too.

After three weeks, try to get the kitten to lap the formula
from your finger and then proceed to encourage "mush" food
eating, as described above. Ask your veterinarian about supplementary pediatric vitamin and mineral drops. These are a
wise investment for kittens who've been deprived of their
mother's nutrients.

Older orphaned kittens can be started on a specialized kitten food, such as Hill's Feline p/d, available with a veterinarian's prescription.

## Kitty Feeding Tips and Other Cautions

1. Don't start your kitten on human food! Once kitty takes
a liking to it, other food will be ignored, and you'll find that
you've created a finicky eater. Kittens grow incredibly fast,

and a quality balanced diet is essential for optimum health. *Treat table scraps as occasional treats—not meals!*

2. Allow your kitten at least one hour after eating before handling, especially by children. (You wouldn't appreciate a piggyback ride on a full stomach, would you?)

3. Be sure the room your kitten or kittens are in is large enough for exercise and free from hazards, such as toxic cleansers, plants, paints, small ingestible objects, and large pets, and also out of the main household traffic area.

4. Sunlight is vital to proper bone and muscle development of young kittens. They should get at least one hour of direct sunlight daily, if possible.

5. Warmth, no matter how much fur those little fluffs of fun have, is necessary. Kittens under five weeks of age without a momma to snuggle into should have an electric heating pad (it must be waterproof) or a heating lamp to keep them warm when sleeping. There should always be enough space, though, for the kitten to move away from the heat when it wants to.

6. If you are feeding your kitten dry food, make sure it's high quality, and not the type that will expand excessively in the kitten's stomach. Test the food by dropping a few bits into a glass of water and seeing how much they expand. You want your pet to feel satisfied, not stuffed.

7. Kittens should *not* look like tiny teddy bears. A sleek, firm, muscular kitten is a healthier kitten and will be a much healthier cat. Avoid meeting their calorie requirements with foods that contain too much cereal filler. Protein provides the most effective, efficient energy during growth.

8. If you want to save time and money by preparing a two-day supply of "mush," store it in an airtight container in the refrigerator. When re-serving, add a little hot water to bring it to room temperature or put the bowl in hot water (as you would a baby's bottle) until the chill is gone. This will enhance the aroma of the food, increase its digestibility, and prevent gastrointestinal upsets that are caused by cold food.

9. Start by feeding four small meals a day. Letting your

kitten get too hungry can cause it to eat too quickly, and more often than not, will result in the unwanted return of that meal to your floor. If you have to be away at work during this period, feed your kitten breakfast laced with about one-fourth teaspoon Karo, maple, or pancake syrup. Whenever a large gap between meals is unavoidable, this will stave off hunger and serve as a helpful energy supplement, but it is not advised as a regular practice. Feed the next meal when you come home and another one before bedtime. If your kitten is able to chew dry food, leave that down—along with fresh water—for meal two and forgo the syrup.

10. At around three months of age, three meals daily (of approximately three ounces of *quality* food at each meal) should fill the needs of most growing kittens.

11. Don't leave food down for more than fifteen to twenty minutes.

12. Don't add bonemeal to your kitten's food. It could upset the proper calcium/phosphorus ratio.

13. Eggshells should not be added to a kitten's diet unless they have been properly cleaned to destroy all possible salmonella contamination.

14. Kittens should not be taken from their mother until they are at least six weeks old.

15. Vaccinations for distemper should be given when kittens are between six and eight weeks of age.

## Shaping Up a Stray the Right Way

*How to turn a scraggly stray into a super cat*

When a stray comes into your life, so can a host of problems—but so can some of the most loving rewards imaginable. Whether you selected the cat from an animal shelter or found it hungry, alone, and looking much like a moth-eaten muff someone tossed in an alley, the moment you bring it home you can begin rectifying its unhappy past and shaping it up for a happy, healthy, and revitalized new life.

*A Safe Start:* If you have other pets at home, don't rush introductions. The wisest thing to do is isolate your new addition for at least a day before you take it to the vet for a thorough professional checkup, which is essential even if you got the cat from an animal shelter. (If the poor waif is obviously in distress, then, of course, take it to a veterinarian immediately.) There are several important reasons for this:

• The cat might be harboring a communicable disease.

• You will have a chance to get acquainted and observe the cat, without dealing with the probable jealousy of other pets and the likely intimidation of your new arrival.

• You'll be able to supply your vet with important diagnostic information by providing a stool sample and reporting any unusual behavior or eating habits.

• If your new pet has any existing health problems or conditions, prompt medical treatment and advice can prevent a lot of heartache. Knowledge of the problems will also allow you to plan a diet that can be tailored specifically to provide your foundling with optimal health. (See chapter 11 for nutritional treatments of common ailments.)

## Important Don'ts

Don't give your stray a bath before it has been examined and you've asked the vet's approval. If the cat is in poor health, which chances are it is, a bath could be extremely dangerous at this time, possibly causing a fatal case of pneumonia. I'd suggest wiping any dirt or excrement off with a warm, damp cloth, then toweling those areas dry immediately.

Don't feed more than a small amount of food at first, no matter how hungry the little guy looks. This is very important. If the cat has worms (a more than likely possibility), a sudden ingestion of food can cause mayhem in the poor creature's gastrointestinal tract and possibly its death. Wait at least two hours after the cat has eaten before offering another small meal.

### FIRST FEEDINGS

Assuming your new family member has no serious problems, starting off with my New-Life Diet is ideal for rapid recuperation from any previous dietary deficiencies, and the best immunity insurance possible for continuous well-being.

Not knowing what the cat has been used to eating can sometimes make starting a new feeding regimen a tricky business. Cats, even hungry ones, can have very definite preferences in food texture and taste, and if addicted to one particular kind may refuse all others—at first.

A change in environment, even if it's for the better, is a stress-inducing situation for a cat, commonly causing it to refuse all food. This might last for a day, even two.

Don't be discouraged, and whatever you do, *don't let your new cat train you!*

NOTE: A food refusal that continues for more than two days warrants veterinary consultation.

Adoptive parents of strays are particularly vulnerable to falling into a "You don't like that? Well, how about this?" syndrome. The result, as I've seen many times, is bewildered owners who can't understand why, after waiting hand and paws upon their pets, their animals look (and are) in such sad shape.

*You're Bigger and Smarter:* Cats, much like children, might know what they like, but what they like is not always what's good for them. If you truly love your pet, the best way to show it is by giving it the gift of fitness through proper feeding.

## The New-Life Health Start Diet for Strays

*This diet is designed for an average eight-pound cat—or one who should weigh that much, give or take a couple of pounds. For the special needs of pregnant and lactating cats; growing kittens; diabetic, geriatric, obese cats; and others with exceptional nutrient requirements or restrictions, consult the Index for individual sections.*

1. Begin by weighing your cat. If ribs and spine are visible, your cat needs a higher daily caloric intake than indicated in chapter 3; if excess flab is present along the abdomen and you can't feel the cat's ribs, a lower daily caloric intake is called for.

2. While you're establishing the quantity of food to feed, you should weigh your cat every week. Since cats aren't dependable for sitting still on a scale, weigh yourself, then weigh yourself holding your cat. The difference in poundage is your cat's weight.

3. Once your cat is at optimal weight, keep the food quality high and adjust the amount fed daily to meet your pet's caloric needs.

4. Every month, after the diet has been established, weigh your cat to see that there isn't a weight loss or gain of more than 5 to 10 percent. If there is, increase or decrease the amount of daily food intake accordingly.

## Getting-Acquainted Basic Breakfast

### Try Dry

Try one quarter to one third cup of professional dry cat food (Iams; Feline Growth, from Hill's; Tamiami, from Beatrice; Super Stars, from Cornucopia). Available from pet stores and vets, these foods supply concentrated energy and nutrition—approximately 125 to 130 calories in just one or two ounces. (Note: An eight-ounce measuring cup holds about three to three-and-one-quarter ounces of dry food.)

If you wish, you can begin with any good-quality commercial dry food, but your new cat will have to consume a larger volume of food to meet its breakfast calorie requirement.

If your new pet refuses dry food and your veterinarian has found no existing dental problem, the cat's refusal could be the result of a prior gum or tooth condition. Then again, it could simply be that the animal has never chewed dry food before. Since dry food is an excellent preventive for tartar buildup and potential dental problems, I feel it should be part of every cat's weekly diet. And the sooner you can get yours to enjoy it, the better.

### How to Get Your Cat to Enjoy Dry Food
- Mix a few pieces of dry food in with the canned.
- Increase the amount of dry as your cat gets accustomed to it, proportionately decreasing the amount of canned. (Don't rush the process.)
- Once your cat will eat a completely dry food meal, feed only dry for three days in a row before offering canned food.

### Breakfast Booster Treats
- Egg yolk or parboiled egg (can be added one to three times weekly)
- Cottage cheese (two tablespoons)
- Plain yogurt (two tablespoons)
- Bacon grease (one-fourth teaspoon, one to three times weekly) but only if you are feeding commercial dry foods

## Deluxe Dinner

### Go Pro
Serve three to four ounces of canned alternative/professional cat food (Feline Growth, from Hill's; Super Stars, from Cornucopia; Tamiami, from Beatrice; Triumph, from Triumph; Total Feline, from Showbound). Refrigerate unused portion. (For optimal flavor retention, store in an airtight container instead of the can.) When re-serving, don't forget to warm to room temperature by adding a little hot water or broth, placing the bowl in a pan of hot water, or setting the bowl in the microwave and reheating the contents until the chill is gone. Test the food's temperature with your finger before feeding. Never recook food and never serve leftover food cold!

It is not advisable to store canned food for more than two days. To avoid waste, I'd suggest serving the remainder of a canned meal the following morning for breakfast and giving dry food for dinner. If the food you're using comes in fifteen-ounce cans, and you find that you still have leftovers, serve it for both meals the next day. The day after that serve only dry food.

### Deluxe Dinner Dividends

• Serve one teaspoon less of leftover canned food and replace with one to two teaspoons cooked chicken, beef, or fish. Limit to three times weekly, since professional foods are optimally balanced, and your goal is optimal nutrition.

• Mix one quarter to one-half teaspoon of brewer's yeast into food. Provides extra B vitamins that can also help keep fleas away.

• If you are not feeding a quality, balanced food regularly, tasty cat vitamins will speed your stray's shape-up. Nutra-Nugget, Vital Nutrition, Felovite, or Fauve are good choices.

## *For Best Results*

Feed no generic or supermarket-label foods.

Comb and brush your pet daily. This helps prevent hair balls, which can cause stomach problems and undermine any nutrition regimen. It will also give you visible evidence of your cat's rapidly improving condition. Buy a comb with teeth spaced widely enough not to pull your cat's fur, yet narrowly enough to remove dead hair, flaky skin, and possible parasite eggs. If mats won't comb out, snip with a blunt scissors. Use a soft bristle brush that will stimulate your pet's oil glands. Brush from tail to neck, neck to tail, then back again.

Your cat might not be able to say how much it appreciates New-Life nutrition, but it will surely show it. (A healthy coat speaks for itself.) Within two weeks the benefits will be obvious; within four they will be irrefutable.

## New-Life for Your Beloved Older Cat

*Just because a cat can't stay young doesn't mean it can't stay healthy.*

Once upon a time, early in my career, I had the good fortune to become acquainted with a cat named Cinderella. She was a beautiful, silvery deep gray, domestic shorthair of magically mixed breed, a combination of kittenish mischief and feline formidability. According to her medical file, she was six years old with no physical problems, and her appearance and behavior gave me no reason to doubt it.

But her file was only partially correct. Cinderella was *sixteen*, not six. The record's inaccuracy was due to a typo; Cinderella's youthfulness was due to her owner's sixteen years of unswerving enlightened nutritional care.

What I learned from this fairy-godmother owner was what I had always believed: Growing old doesn't have to mean looking or feeling old. Recognizing that a cat's nutritional needs vary with age—as well as breed, physical condition, household environment, even changes in weather—is necessary for keeping your pet in optimal condition.

*How Old Is Old?* A cat that celebrates its tenth birthday, or any thereafter, by bounding effortlessly up on the counter for a preview of dinner is not one that you might deem old; but, visible or not, aging changes have begun. Dietary modifications must be considered if you want your pet to continue celebrating birthdays in equivalent good health.

Not all cats age at the same rate or in the same fashion, but with increasing years all will experience the effects of aging. The aging process cannot be stopped, but it can be slowed down with good preventive nutrition.

Familiarizing yourself with changes and resulting problems that can occur with aging will help you decide what food adjustments are best for your individual cat.

As your cat ages:

| CHANGES | POSSIBLE PROBLEMS |
| --- | --- |
| Decreased thyroid function and basal metabolism | Obesity, due to lowered energy needs and slowing down of all body functions |
| Decreased sense of smell | Appetite loss, weight loss, diminished intake of vital nutrients |
| Decreased sensitivity to thirst | Dehydration, kidney disease |
| Decreased ability to regulate body temperature for warmth or cooling | Increased susceptibility to illness |
| Decreased immune-system effectiveness | Increased susceptibility to illness, atrophy, and tumors in reproductive organs of males and females |
| Decreased liver function | Increased susceptibility to toxins; diminished drug tolerance and ability to properly digest and utilize necessary fats |
| Decreased pancreas function | Impaired food digestion and assimilation, gastrointestinal upsets, increased chances of diabetes mellitus |
| Tooth and gum degeneration | Insufficient food intake because of impaired chewing ability, vomiting, constipation, gum tumors |

| CHANGES | POSSIBLE PROBLEMS |
|---|---|
| Decreased salivary secretion | Insufficient nutrient intake, vomiting, constipation |
| Decreased restful sleep | Unexplained irritability and other behavioral quirks |
| Decreased visual and hearing acuity | Irritability, increased susceptibility to environmental hazards, increased stress, vomiting and loss of equilibrium due to inner-ear degeneration |
| Decreased intestinal absorption | Insufficient intake of all nutrients, calcium deficiency causing osteoporosis (brittle bones), gas, diarrhea, constipation, odorous stools |
| Decreased colon motility | Constipation |
| Decreased skin elasticity; drying, thinning, and coarsening of coat; excessive or decreased production of oil glands | Increased susceptibility to skin diseases |
| Decreased kidney (renal) function | Generalized kidney disease (see chapter 11), gastric ulcers, excessive drinking and urination, incontinence |
| Muscular-skeletal degeneration | Flaccid abdominal and other visible muscles as well as cardiac (heart) muscles, arthritis, back stiffness, poor coordination of limbs |

| CHANGES | POSSIBLE PROBLEMS |
|---|---|
| Decreased cardiovascular function | Heart disease (see chapter 11), arteriosclerosis, easily fatigued |
| Decreased respiratory function | Chronic bronchitis, emphysema, tumors in respiratory system, asthma, fatigue |
| Decreased neurological function | Slow response to stimuli, memory loss, impaired sensory reactions (sight, sound, smell, taste), nervousness, irritability |

## New Ways to Feed and Nurture an Older Cat

• Feed smaller, easily digested, quality, balanced, high-BV-protein meals more frequently, three or four times daily. This eases the stress on internal organs, and keeps the immune system strong and your pet's energy level from falling.

• Avoid all generic foods.

• Avoid feeding meals with imbalanced essential fatty acids or those with incorrect or insufficient nutrients to utilize fat. This can prevent flaking, dry skin, and a wide variety of coat and skin problems. Supplements such as Mirracoat, Vital Nutrition, Pet Tabs F.A., and any others that contain vitamin A, vitamin E, choline, and balanced arachidonic, linoleic, and linolenic fatty acids can help. Note: Always read the supplement label to make sure that *all* necessary fatty acids are included.

• Count calories and make those calories count—a fat cat is not going to be a fit cat.

• Don't feed your cat baby food. The calcium/phosphorus ratio is wrong for felines and can worsen many health problems.

• Brush your older pet daily and give hair-ball medication two or three times a week.

• Make sure your cat has fresh water every day—and drinks it. Dehydration is not uncommon in older cats because of their decreased thirst sensitivity. If you find that your cat isn't drinking, add a bit of water (or warm broth, clam juice, or tomato juice) to the animal's meals.

• As cats grow older, their calcium needs increase. A deficiency can cause brittle bones (osteoporosis). Adding sardines to your pet's diet (provided the cat doesn't have FUS) is a way to provide extra calcium that even finicky eaters appreciate. Mash the sardines before adding to your pet's food, and remember that the addition shouldn't be more than 25 percent of the meal. Cottage cheese is another easy-to-enjoy calcium booster for older cats.

• Brewer's yeast with bran (which contains the B complex vitamins and fiber) and vitamin C (200 to 500 mg) are excellent stress fighters and constipation preventives. I recommend supplementing an older cat's diet with both daily. (If using the powered form of vitamin C, one eighth teaspoon is approximately 500 mg.) Bee pollen, which can be purchased at most health food stores, is another fine daily addition.

• If your pet is not eating a quality alternative food, I'd recommend giving a multiple vitamin-mineral supplement (such as Vital Nutrition or Nutra Nuggets) daily. CAUTION: If your cat has any existing medical problems, check with your vet before making any dietary additions or changes.

• A little extra attention goes a long way in keeping a cat youthful, especially if you give that attention in the form of exercise play. The exercise should not, of course, be excessive or exhausting. My twelve-year-old rex, Jeddy, loves stalking and swatting bubbles and pursuing any toy that rolls downstairs. And you'll be surprised at how short walks can work energizing wonders.

• Because older cats are often candidates for respiratory problems, keeping a humidifier in your home during the winter months is advisable.

• Don't forget about sunlight! It plays an important part in the well-being of cats of all ages and is particularly important for older ones. Sunlight provides vitamin D, which is vital for bone growth and maintenance as well as effective metabolization of calcium. If you have an indoor cat, be aware that ordinary glass windows do not let in the essential ultraviolet rays. There are, though, special types of plastic windows that do. Your local hardware store should be able to tell you about them. You can also buy a special "full spectrum" artificial light that provides a close equivalent to natural sunlight.

## SUPER SUPPER PICKER-UPPER FOR SENIOR CATS

*A special once-or-twice-a-week treat created for pampering your pet*

2–3 ounces cooked chicken (no skin) or boneless fish (haddock, sole, flounder)
1 tablespoon coarse bran
⅛ teaspoon brewer's yeast
1 eggshell, *cooked* and finely ground, or 1 pulverized 50-mg calcium tablet
⅛ teaspoon wheat germ oil
1 tablespoon cottage cheese
1 tablespoon cooked oatmeal

Mix all ingredients well. If cat prefers a more moist consistency, add 1–2 tablespoons of water or warm broth. (Approximately 180 calories.)

## Questions and Answers About Feeding for Fitness

### TEETH 'N' PROBLEMS

*I found a stray, about six years old, who has no teeth. I've been feeding her only canned food, but when I give my other two cats dry food, my toothless stray wants some. Is it all right for her to have it?*

It's not only all right, it's probably one of the best things you can do for her. Though she has no visible teeth, she might still have molars, and chewing dry food can at least keep *them* healthy. In fact, you should encourage her eating dry food for just this reason.

Any cats denied dry food, or an equivalent tartar remover and gum stimulant, are prime candidates for tooth decay and loss (which your stray obviously was). But it's never too late to start on recuperative dental health. No, teeth won't grow back, but dry food can stimulate gums enough to prevent gingivitis and other periodontal problems. If at first the food is too difficult for your cat to chew, moisten it a bit with water or broth and then gradually decrease the amount of liquid until the food is completely dry. Once your stray is eating it, keep feeding it at least three to five times weekly. I'd also advise giving a vitamin C supplement, 100 to 200 mg daily, to help counteract gum degeneration.

You should be prepared, nonetheless, to face the fact that her interest in dry food and capacity to eat it properly might be two different things, in which case serving it in anything but a softened form is inadvisable. Cats eat with their tongues, and if your stray takes to gulping down the food without chewing, you'll soon find it coming back up. If this happens, you're better off serving her a quality, alternative canned food, with high-BV protein, fat, vitamins, and caloric density, so she'll be able to get maximum nutrition from minimal portions. Keep up the vitamin C supplements, and two or three times a week substitute moistened dry food for a quarter of her canned food so she won't feel left out. Of course, if she eventually does become able to chew dry food, proceed as I've described above.

# *Special Needs of Special Breeds*

✧❀✧❀✧❀✧❀

The following food and supplement recommendations are not intended to be prescriptive. Before making changes in your cat's diet, consult your veterinarian to be sure that your pet has no special physical problems, or is taking no medication that might contraindicate alterations in the animal's present diet.

### *Abyssinian*

Shorthaired, firm, and muscular, this lithe and fast-moving cat with the exotic look of an ancient Egyptian animal god is known for its sleek, shiny coat and unbounded playfulness. Its diet *must* contain ample protein and balanced fatty acids to meet high-energy requirements and maintain coat in good condition.

Many Abyssinians are prone to gingivitis, so I recommend feeding a quality alternative dry food at least three to five times a week to help prevent tartar buildup and keep gums healthy, as well as giving vitamin C, 50 to 75 mg, every day.

If you are using generic or supermarket-label food, add a good fatty-acid supplement (containing all essential fatty acids and balanced vitamins and minerals) to one meal daily.

### American Shorthair

The classic, tough, sturdy alley cat is big in size and has an appetite to match. Optimally, these cats should be rounded and robust, firm and not flabby. Unfortunately, obesity is all too common in the breed.

To prevent your American shorthair from becoming a flabby tabby, once a month gently pinch its sides. You should always be able to feel the cat's ribs without difficulty. If you can't, a calorie cutback is in order. Avoid feeding this lusty feline any foods with a high cereal content, don't leave meals down all day, and skip the bedtime snacks.

### American Wirehair

Because of the breed's lightly curled, springy coat, it's important that this cat's hair grows evenly—unless, of course, you don't mind living with an animal that will look like a used Brillo pad on paws. Since the coat is the first area to show nutritional deficiencies, a balanced diet is essential. (See chapter 10.)

Avoid feeding table scraps and treat foods that could interfere with the wirehair's intake of quality protein and fat.

### Balinese and Javanese

Longhaired and active, these elegant and inquisitive felines require frequent brushing. They're also high-spirited (occasionally *too* high) and use up their B vitamins faster than you can name them. A simple remedy is to add one eighth to one quarter teaspoon of brewer's yeast to their meals. I'd also advise vitamin C, 50 to 100 mg, as a routine daily supplement.

To help prevent dull, cottonlike coats (a frequent problem) as well as dry, flaking skin, they should receive a balanced fatty-acid supplement with zinc once a day. Bee pollen, available at health food stores, is a fine powder, usually in capsules that can be opened easily and mixed with food. It's high in vitamins $B_{12}$, E, and K, great for skin health, and also acts as an antibacterial agent.

Hair-ball medication should be given two to three times weekly, between meals.

### Birman

This large, pensive, silky-haired cat with white-gloved paws loves company; to look and feel its best when socializing, it should be kept in proper condition.

Essential fatty acids are a must, along with sufficient vitamin E in the diet to utilize them. If you're not providing a high-protein, high-fat alternative/professional food, supplement meals with a quarter teaspoon bacon grease or, preferably, a balanced store-bought fatty-acid formula with zinc. I'd also recommend adding the powder from one bee pollen capsule to one meal a day.

A diet that promotes steady, firm growth from kittenhood will keep your Birman muscular instead of fat—and sleek for life.

### Bombay

Of medium size, this muscular extrovert's most outstanding feature is its soft, glossy coat. Complete and balanced foods, with high-BV protein, all the essential fatty acids, and zinc are daily diet necessities. But watch out! The Bombay enjoys its meals and has a tendency to overeat. Feed it quality, not quantity.

If you're serving supermarket/commercial food, you should also provide a balanced fatty-acid supplement with vitamins and minerals daily.

### British Shorthair

Large and placid, with an impressive thick coat, a British shorthair's favorite pastimes are sleeping and eating. Since this breed's relatively inactive life-style is conducive to obesity and FUS, maximum nutrition must be provided in minimum quantity.

Feed only twice daily. Do not leave food out for all-day nibbling.

Avoid feeding red fish and foods high in magnesium. (See chapter 4 for low-magnesium foods.)

Always keep fresh water available.

If you're not providing a quality alternative/professional diet, I'd suggest giving a balanced fatty-acid supplement with zinc once a day.

Vitamin C, 200 to 500 mg daily, will help keep urine acidic and can aid in the prevention of FUS. Time-release pills are recommended. (See chapter 2 for cautions on administering ascorbic acid.)

Add tomato juice to moist food when possible. Avoid feeding sardines, anchovies, herring, and sweetbreads.

### Burmese

An active show-off, with a stunning sable brown coat that any feline would envy, the Burmese is a combination stand-up (and roll-over) comic and Olympic athlete.

The breed is prone to ocular discharge, so supplementing the diet with vitamin C, 200 to 500 mg daily, is recommended. I've found this helpful in averting potential eye problems and clearing up those that exist.

For continued coat beauty, give your Burmese a balanced fatty-acid supplement with zinc daily, along with the powder from one bee pollen capsule, which can easily be mixed with food.

## Chartreux

The large, gentle powerhouse of a cat, the Chartreux is a smiler, a jumper, a hunter, and great for multi-pet households. Its thick bluish coat is plush and should glisten. Though capable of numerous activities, it has a tendency to be lazy and often enjoys entire afternoons just sunbathing.

Coat should be shiny, not at all dull. If the cat isn't being fed an alternative/professional food, give it a balanced fatty-acid supplement with zinc daily.

Do not overfeed. Once a month, gently pinch your pet's side to be sure you can still feel its ribs. A Chartreux can easily become very chubby.

Feed low-magnesium foods. Incidence of FUS is frequent. Add one to two tablespoons of tomato juice to moist food three to five times weekly and supplement the diet with 200 to 500 mg of time-release vitamin C daily.

## Colorpoint Shorthair

Essentially, and for all nutritional purposes, this breed is Siamese with color variations. (See Siamese below.)

## Cornish Rex

A curvy cat, structured somewhat like a small greyhound, whose wavy, plush, rippled coat makes it an eye-catching pet. Active and energetic, the Cornish rex, because its coat lacks guard hairs, produces little dander and is ideal for owners who might be allergic to other cats. It still sheds, though, so hairball medication should be given one to two times a week.

These cats have a high metabolism (their normal body temperature is above that of other breeds) and huge appetites. Do not allow free feeding! As energetic as the Cornish rex is, it can easily overeat and become a blimp. It needs food with quality protein and usable fat for meeting its energy needs as well as keeping warm, particularly the latter. This breed is not meant for cold climates or cold weather. I recommend keeping a T-shirt on a Rex from October to May.

The tail area has a tendency to become oily if the diet is insufficient in usable fat and vitamin E. Brush the coat with a *soft* brush—but do it gently and only occasionally.

If you're not feeding your rex an alternative/professional food, I would suggest the following immune-system fortifiers.

• A multivitamin-mineral supplement five times weekly (Fauve, Vital Nutrition). If using a people supplement, give the pediatric dosage.

• A daily fatty-acid food supplement containing all essential fatty acids plus vitamins A, D, E, selenium, and zinc.

• Extra vitamin C, 200 to 500 mg daily.

• Vitamin B complex, balanced, 25 to 50 mg daily, or a quarter teaspoon brewer's yeast mixed with food.

## Cymric

The long and short of this cat are its hair (long) and its front legs (short). It has no tail to speak of—and shouldn't—since it is the longhaired version of the distinctly tailless Manx breed, from which it descended.

Calcium is an important dietary nutrient because of the Cymric's unusual body symmetry—raised muscular hindquarters, short front legs—and should always be supplied in an equal or 2:1 ratio with phosphorus. Substituing a quarter cup of cottage or ricotta cheese for 25 percent of a Cymric's meal three to five times weekly is a simple and an effective way to slip in extra calcium.

All-meat diets are a definite *no!* The high phosphorus/calcium ratio can be particularly detrimental to a Cymric's health.

Quality high-BV protein and balanced fatty acids are necessary for adequate muscle growth and keeping this cat's double coat shining. If you're not feeding an alternative/professional food regularly, a balanced fatty-acid supplement with zinc should be given daily.

Brush and comb your Cymric two or three times a week. Give hair-ball medication twice weekly (between meals).

### Devon Rex

A slightly larger, fuzzier, longer-haired, but more delicate version of the Cornish rex (see above). The same high-fat-quality protein, protective warmth, and supplement needs apply.

### Egyptian Mau

This muscular and stealthy predator is a hardy, medium-sized shorthair with a slick, spotted, leopardlike coat. Its nutritional needs are basic and met easily with a well-balanced feline diet (see chapter 10).

A complete fatty-acid supplement with zinc given five times weekly will keep its coat in top condition, and one eighth to one quarter teaspoon brewer's yeast (mixed with meals) can prevent B vitamin insufficiencies, which sometimes are the cause of this breed's occasional, inexplicable unsociable behavior.

### Exotic Shorthair

If you can imagine a sort of low-maintenance, laid-back, shorthaired Persian, you've a pretty good idea of an exotic shorthair. This cat is easier to groom than a Persian, but sufficient balanced fatty acids and a high-BV-protein diet are nonetheless essential for the health of its lush fur coat.

Like Persians, exotic shorthairs are prone to eye discharge and infections. It's therefore advisable to supply them with 200 to 500 mg of extra vitamin C daily. I'd also suggest giving a dietary supplement that includes a minimum of 1,250 IU of vitamin A, a balanced B complex (with at least 100 mcg of $B_6$ and 4 mcg of $B_{12}$), 15 mcg of selenium, and 12 mg of zinc at least five times weekly.

## Havana Brown

A hardy, adaptable cat that is full of fun and plays very well with others, but has a tendency to want its owner's undivided attention. It has many character and physical traits of a Siamese.

The Havana's shorthair coat requires minimal grooming (once a week is fine), but to keep it lustrous, this cat should be given a balanced fatty-acid supplement with vitamins and minerals daily.

## Himalayan and Kashmir

Gentle, longhaired Persian types, these cats like to exercise; they do well in roomy homes with other pets and children.

Himalayans and Kashmirs tend to have improperly developed tear ducts, causing discharge from the eyes. Because of their short noses, they're also more susceptible to respiratory disease. Vitamin C, 200 to 500 mg, should be given on a daily basis. A balanced fatty-acid supplement, containing at least 1,250 IU of vitamin A, 70 IU of vitamin E, 15 mcg of selenium, and 12 mg of zinc, should be given five times weekly.

Conscientious daily coat combing is necessary to prevent tangled, cottony-looking fur, and hair-ball medication should be given two or three times weekly (between meals).

## Japanese Bobtail

Usually calico-patterned (red, black, and white), this unique feline—immortalized for centuries in Japanese artworks—is both reserved and playful. In fact, on a warm summer day, a bob (as it's often called) might even climb into a birdbath or shallow tub for a recreational splash. Unfortunately, I can't recommend the bob as a pet for young children. Its tail, which is short, curled, densely furred, and looks more like something that belongs on a bunny than a cat, is very, *very* sensitive. Incorrect fondling can cause this animal great pain, sometimes to the extent that it will flee from all future stroking.

Easy to care for, your bob only really needs a balanced diet of alternative/professional food and a mineral supplement as a general immune-system booster to keep in shape.

## Korat

If you're looking for an alert "guard cat," a well-bred Korat can't be beat. Properly aloof and often suspicious of strangers, this shorthair, with its extraordinary agility and fabulous silver blue coat, is a regular James (or Jane) Bond on paws, and devoted to its owners.

Korats deserve nothing but the best in the way of nutrition, and they should get it—on schedule. Feed alternative/professional food regularly, with a daily vitamin C supplement of 100 to 200 mg.

If you are providing supermarket/commercial foods, increase the vitamin C to 200 to 500 mg daily (Korats are susceptible to respiratory infections). I also suggest giving your pet a balanced fatty-acid supplement with vitamins and minerals at least five times weekly.

## Maine Coon

At first glance, you might think it's a dog in drag, and with good reason. This is a *large* cat. At ten months my Maine coon nephew, George, was nineteen pounds of muscular machismo and had taken a lion's share of awards at the Empire Cat Show.

My advice for keeping a Maine coon in keen shape is to feed it high-BV-protein balanced meals three to four times daily. A concentrated alternative dry food is recommended. This will supply correctly proportioned amounts of energy, keeping the cat muscular and active. You do *not* want a fat Maine coon, believe me. Obesity problems aside, you could get a hernia just carrying it to the vet.

I'd like to add that as big as Maine coons are, they are gentle, loving, adaptable to all sorts of household situations and climates, and make terrific pets. A regular weekly combing should be enough to keep their coats tangle-free.

## Malayan

A purebred Malayan is a bit more assertive than a Burmese, but their nutritional needs are the same. (See Burmese above.)

## Manx

Though of medium size, this tailless, wily cat is deceptively powerful. Its awkward gait and build are genetic, not caused by a nutritional deficiency.

The Manx's thick double coat needs regular brushing and a good fatty-acid supplement with zinc five times weekly to keep it glossy. If you are not feeding it a quality high-BV-protein food, the supplement should be given daily.

Personality-wise, a Manx is a one-person pet, perfect for single owners.

## Norwegian Forest Cat

If cats could ski, the Norwegian Forest cat would be the first on the slopes, and undoubtedly—because it thrives on companionship—a hit at the ski lodge.

Its double-thick coat is not only beautiful but water-resistant and will stay tangle-free. I'd recommend occasional combing, though, to slough off dead hair and cells, which will help prevent hair balls as well as stimulate the oil glands that keep the coat water-resistant. Bathing is not advised; it can wash off those oils.

Make sure this cat is eating a balanced diet of high-BV protein, getting a quality fatty-acid vitamin supplement with zinc daily, and hair-ball medication (between meals) twice weekly.

## Ocicat

This large, imposing, sleek shorthair has the look of a feral feline, but is in every sense of the word a pussycat—sweet, bright, and gentle.

This is essentially a very healthy cat and is easily kept that way by avoiding food with too much cereal filler and sticking to a high-BV-protein diet.

Ocicats are, however, prone to nervousness. Supplementing their diet with B complex vitamins—one eighth to one quarter teaspoon brewer's yeast mixed with food daily—is the simplest preventive and cure I've found for their jitters.

## Oriental Shorthair

Distinctively elegant, agile, and loving, the Oriental is a thinner, more muscular, almost-identical twin to the Siamese. Not surprisingly, the two breeds have the same nutritional needs. These are listed in detail under "Siamese" below.

## Persian

The Persian is the quintessential, luxuriously longhaired, and usually royally pampered lap cat. Unfortunately, many of the Persians I've seen have been pampered to death by indulgent but nutritionally uneducated owners.

The major errors, I've found, are feeding all-meat diets, overfeeding with table scraps and treats, and leaving food down for all-day nibbling. These are definite—and dangerous—no-nos! (See chapter 3 for explanations of these meal-time mistakes.)

Persians are not particularly active cats and are prone to obesity and FUS; proper diet is therefore a necessity. Calorie intake should be controlled and only low-magnesium foods fed. Do not leave food down all day, because after eating, a cat's urine becomes more alkaline, a danger for those pre-disposed to FUS.

Ocular discharge is common in this breed, so you should clean a Persian's eyes once or twice daily with a piece of damp, sterile cotton. To prevent eye infections, a strong immune system must be present to provide ample antibodies. Vitamin C, 200 to 500 mg (time-release pills preferred), should be given daily. Also, a balanced fatty-acid vitamin-mineral supplement containing vitamins A, E, and D, selenium, and zinc will help boost natural defenses while keeping a Persian's coat in shape. If you're feeding supermarket/commercial food, give the supplement daily. A bee pollen capsule, which can be opened and mixed with food, is another wise supplement for keeping skin and fur in super shape.

With Persians, grooming cannot be ignored and should be done daily. Remember, when brushing, brush backward to distribute oils evenly. Administer hair-ball medication between meals two or three times weekly.

## Ragdoll

Related to the Persian, this exceptionally large longhaired cat is happiest when not in motion. To call it mellow is an understatement; to arouse its interest in anything other than food or sleep is an achievement. Despite its size, it's the perfect pet for small apartments.

Nutritionally, the ragdoll's needs are the same as a Persian's (see above), but you'll find that it requires considerably less grooming because its coat doesn't mat as easily. Hair-ball medication should be given between meals two or three times weekly.

## Russian Blue

A svelte, aloof shorthair, this cat sports a lush double-thick coat that often conceals excess pounds if feeding isn't carefully supervised. The Russian blue tends to lounge more than leap, making it an easy target for obesity and FUS.

Supermarket/commercial foods should be kept to a minimum. You don't want to dull this cat's exquisite fur. Brush it backward, then forward daily. This will stimulate oil glands, remove dead hair, and keep the coat shiny without flattening it. Give hair-ball medication between meals once or twice a week.

If you're not providing an alternative/professional diet regularly, give a balanced fatty-acid supplement with vitamins and minerals every day.

Though this breed is usually gentle, I've seen quite a few unruly Russian blue exceptions. If yours is one, I'd suggest supplementing its meals with a balanced 25 to 50 mg B complex and mixing one to two tablespoons of chamomile tea in moist food daily. Start with one teaspoon and gradually increase the amount.

## Scottish Fold

Known for its folded-down ears and soulful eyes, this well-behaved and amiable cat is surprisingly hardy. Feeding yours a good balanced diet of high-BV protein and fat can keep it that way.

I would suggest, though, that since the Scottish fold is particularly susceptible to ear mites, you supplement its daily diet with brewer's yeast (one eighth to one quarter teaspoon), vitamin C (150 to 200 mg), and a pinch of garlic. If ear mites are present, you'll need special medication from the vet to kill them. In any event, cleaning your cat's ears once a week with a cotton swab dampened in a mild hydrogen peroxide solution is a must for averting serious potential problems.

## Siamese

The Siamese is unquestionably the cat most likely to want things its own way—and usually to get them. Incredibly intelligent, ingenious, agile, and active, this dauntless, ultrasleek, and slender feline has a mind of its own, and you never know what it will think of next.

To meet its high-energy needs and still retain its long, lean beauty (a show Siamese must have absolutely minimal fat and muscle over its rib cage), this cat requires high-BV protein and balanced fatty acids daily. Commercial foods with a high cereal or carbohydrate content should be avoided, as should raw-meat diets (these can cause muscle flaccidity and hair loss). On the other hand, nondigestible carbohydrates (fiber), such as beet pulp or grated carrots, should be included in your Siamese's diet to cleanse intestine walls and prevent bowel problems. If there is a fiber insufficiency, you'll soon find your little genius rectifying it by chewing up socks, sweatshirts, towels, and so on.

For a very active Siamese, a little nutritional calming down can be obtained by supplementing the diet with a balanced vitamin B complex, 50 to 75 mg, or one eighth to one quarter teaspoon brewer's yeast daily. I'd recommend that you give vitamin C, 150 to 200 mg, along with it. If your cat seems really hyper, offer—or mix with food—some chamomile tea (room temperature) in the evening.

## Singapura

Small and shorthaired, this breed is very similar to the Abyssinian (see above). A Singapura does, though, require a diet high in potassium iodide (iodine), which influences the proper function of the thyroid gland. Most alternative and quality commercial foods contain adequate amounts of this mineral (check labels), but if you are supplying a homemade diet I'd suggest you supplement your pet's meals with kelp, which is available in health food stores. (Remember: Whenever giving people supplements to cats, always use recommended pediatric dosage.)

### Snowshoe

This breed is not quite as large as a Maine coon (see above), but it has the same basic temperament, sociability, fortitude, and nutritional needs.

### Somali

An active and often acrobatic longhair whose theme song is "Don't Fence Me In," this fun-loving feline likes room to play.

A Somali needs high-BV protein and quality fat. If you're not feeding yours an alternative/professional food, give it a balanced fatty-acid supplement with vitamins and minerals daily, as well as an egg yolk (no uncooked white) twice weekly.

Many Somalis have a tendency to be hyper as well as active—usually in the evening when you're ready for sleep. If yours is a late-night partier, a vitamin B complex, 50 to 75 mg, or one eighth to one quarter teaspoon brewer's yeast is a smart daily meal supplement, along with a nightcap of room-temperature chamomile tea.

### Sphynx

A fabulous, fragile feline, virtually hairless, the Sphynx needs special care and clothing (it must wear a sweater or T-shirt at all times) and requires a truly dedicated owner, who will not only protect it from the cold but provide it with absolutely optimal nutrition—at least four times a day! Because of this cat's extra-high metabolism, obesity isn't a problem, but supplying adequate nutrition is.

A balanced fatty-acid supplement (including vitamins A, D, and E, selenium, and zinc), vitamin C (150 to 250 mg), and a balanced B complex (50 to 100 mg) should be given daily. A raw egg yolk (not white) can be added to meals two or three times a week.

## Tiffany

This is the longhaired version of a Burmese (see above). Their nutritional needs are the same, though the Tiffany requires more grooming and should get hair-ball medication between meals once or twice a week.

## Tonkinese

A delightful, mischievous, quality combination of Siamese and Burmese, the Tonkinese has basically the same nutritional and supplement needs as both the Siamese and the Burmese (see listings above), but tends to eat more than either. Obesity can cause your Tonkinese serious problems, so be careful not to overfeed.

Also keep in mind that a Tonkinese, like a Siamese, has a definite intestine-cleansing need for fiber. If there are fiber insufficiencies in your pet's diet, you're likely to find that there will be insufficiencies in your sweaters, socks, and towels as well.

## Turkish Angora

This tall feline is a sociable, trainable, longhaired beauty that enjoys hunting, playing, and even taking a splash in the tub now and then.

High-BV protein and fat are diet essentials, as is a good daily vitamin B complex supplement and 150 to 200 mg of time-release vitamin C. Dry food should be provided at least three times weekly to keep teeth and gums in good condition. Give hair-ball medication two or three times a week between meals.

Avoid giving your pet foods with dyes in them. These can discolor your cat's mane.

## Questions and Answers
## About Special Needs of Special Breeds

### SHAPING UP A SIAMESE FOR SHOW

*My Siamese, Shadow, is in perfect physical shape and health, but I've been told that if I want to enter him in a show he should be thinner. Is there any nutritionally safe, short-term way to slim him down?*

Yes, there is. Two days before a show, feed Shadow just a quarter cup of boiled chicken (no skin) or boiled fish for breakfast and dinner, along with a balanced vitamin B complex supplement and 100 mg of vitamin C. He might not be thrilled with the dietary change, but it's only for two days. He'll lose about a pound and gain that extreme lean, tubular line that judges look for in a prize-winning Siamese.

### HAIRLESS EARS FEARS

*Three months ago, I was given a dark, reddish brown, altered male cat that I was told was a purebred domestic shorthair with no health problems. He's playful, loves to climb on my shoulder, has a fine shiny coat, and looks physically fit—except he has no hair on his ears. Have you any idea what could be causing this?*

My guess would be genetics. If your pet is indeed a purebred domestic shorthair, it's probably a Havana brown, a breed with naturally hairless ears.

### SNUFFING SNEEZES

*I was never allergic to cats, but whenever I'm around my boyfriend's Persian I get a runny nose and sneeze a lot. Do Persian cats have more dander than others? Is there any way to reduce it through diet?*

I'm surprised that it's a Persian that is affecting you. Long-haired cats usually shed hair in clumps, while shorthaired breeds shed small hairs that float around in the air easily, and are generally more irritating to susceptible individuals. But if your boyfriend's Persian has a poor coat or flaking skin, this could be what's causing your problem.

I'd suggest you evaluate the cat's diet and make sure it contains ample vitamins A and E and high-BV protein. These improve coat and skin and reduce shedding. Also try bathing the cat once a month in a solution of a half cup fabric softener and a half cup tepid water. This will coat the hair and help keep it from flying—and, hopefully, your nose from running. (You also might consider buying an air filter for your boyfriend's apartment.)

# PART THREE

# *Getting Better All the Time*

# 7

# *Getting Physical*

❖❀❖❀❖❀❖❀

## The Home Health Checkup

*Giving your cat a simple monthly examination can prevent potential problems for years.*

We all have a tendency to take our pets for granted, but you're making a big mistake if you do so. Cat owners, in particular, share the erroneous belief that their four-footed companions know what's best for them and rarely think about their pet's diet or health until the animal becomes visibly ill.

The truth is, smart as cats are, you're smarter. With minimal effort—essentially a once-a-month home examination—you can avert a variety of problems and unnecessary trips to the vet, and keep your cat as fit as it ought to be—for life.

## The Quick Cat Scan

1. Have you noticed any recent changes in your cat's attitude or behavior, such as listlessness, restlessness, loss of appetite, aggression?

2. Does your pet's coat look dull? Feel dry, brittle, or greasy?

3. Are its whiskers short or broken?

4. Using your hand, brush the cat's hair backward from tail to head. Its skin should be a normal grayish white. The tail area should not be greasy or have sparse hair. Check for any patches of flaking, reddened, or irritated skin. Also look carefully for fleas or any little black flecks (the excrete of fleas) on skin.

5. Does the neck, back, or base of the tail show any lesions?

6. Smell your hand after running it through your cat's fur. Your fingers should not have an unpleasant, fishy, rancid odor.

7. Are you able to feel good muscle tone around the sternum (breastbone)? It should not be soft or flaccid.

8. Do you feel a firm muscle mass with you run your hand down the cat's spine and over the rib cage?

9. Open your cat's mouth and smell its breath. It should smell clean and not have an offensive odor.

10. Look at the gums. They should not be pale or white; nor should they be swollen, bright red, or bleeding.

11. Check the teeth. They should be free of tartar and not loose.

12. Examine the cat's eyes. Are they clear of film and free of mucous discharge? Is there any crusting around them?

13. Feel the inner side of your cat's thighs. Are there any roundish bumps or swellings? These indicate enlarged lymph nodes and usually the presence of worms.

14. Is your pet's stomach unusually distended?

15. Look at the paw pads. They should be smooth (or leathery for outdoor cats) and not cracked.

16. Examine your cat's nails. They should not be brittle or split.

17. Check the ears. They should not be sensitive to touch or have a foul-smelling odor. Look inside for black, crusty matter; this is usually a sign of ear mites, which require veterinary medication.

If your cat scores poorly on its monthly health scan, it's time to pay more attention to what your pet has been eating. (Review "Avoiding Nutritional Cat-astrophes" in chapter 1.)

## Simple Symptoms Can Be Serious

*Ignoring minor symptoms could mean courting major illnesses.*

Just because your cat's symptoms have nutritional connections doesn't mean it's safe to assume there's no need for medical attention. Nutrients can work wonders, but there might be times when you need miracles that only proper medication and professional treatment can provide. Here is a brief review of what health problems various symptoms might indicate.

*Symptoms:* Pale gums and tongue, listlessness, appetite loss, mood changes, diarrhea, vomiting, coughing.

*Possible Ailments:* Anemia, which is often caused by simple parasite infestation, but also a potential indication of coccidiosis, enteritis, tumors, liver damage, steatitis, chronic nephritis, poison, fungus infections, feline leukemia, or distemper. If you suspect anemia, a veterinary diagnosis of its cause is essential so that correct medication and treatment can be started as soon as possible. Unless contraindicated, a diet of high-BV protein (liver and meat) with iron and vitamin supplements is recommended. Ask your vet to prescribe the dosages, since different cats, conditions, and prescription diets will require different amounts.

*Symptoms:* Swollen or distended abdomen, restlessness.

*Possible Ailments:* Bloat, excessive gas often caused by eating large amounts of food too quickly or the ingestion of a foreign body. If distress is acute, immediate veterinary treatment is essential to prevent rupture of the animal's stomach. Metritis, a chronic or acute uterine infection in queens, often life-threatening, is evidenced by a swollen, distended abdomen, though listlessness, as opposed to restlessness, usually accompanies this condition. Prompt veterinary treatment is vital.

*Symptoms:* Excessive or thick eye discharge, film over eyes.

*Possible Ailments:* Irritation due to dust or smoke. Washing the cat's eyes twice daily with a piece of sterile cotton that's been dipped into a warm, mild boric-acid solution should clear this up within a day or two. If not, the cause could be an ulcer, a scratch on the cornea, a foreign body lodged in the eye, conjunctivitis, or a signal of disease in another part of the body, often just worms, but possibly a much more serious condition. In any event, professional diagnois and treatment are called for. With all eye ailments, I'd recommend a raw egg yolk be fed at least once a week and a balanced fatty-acid supplement with vitamin A and zinc be added to the cat's meals five times weekly—unless contraindicated because of medication or special treatment—until the condition has cleared up.

*Symptoms:* Vomiting, diarrhea, loss of appetite, matted fur, a film over the eyes.

*Possible Ailments:* Feline infectious enteritis (distemper), an extremely contagious viral disease that can be prevented by vaccination and annual booster shots; if untreated, it will often permanently impair eyesight and can be fatal. Also possibly indicated is colitis (chronic enteritis), an inflammation of the large intestine that tends to recur in stressed or allergy-prone cats. A bland diet, such as cooked lean lamb and rice, is advised for at least two weeks. Supermarket/commercial cat foods should be avoided. (See "Allergies" in chapter 11.)

*Symptoms:* Dry, scaly skin; itching.
*Possible Ailments:* Follicular dermatitis, often caused by a dietary or hormonal imbalance; it can also be a symptom of nephritis, a kidney disorder, or an underactive thyroid gland.

## Emergency Treatments

*When a crisis occurs, there's no time to think—so just know what to do.*

### Emetics

*To induce vomiting when poisoning is suspected:*
Mix one teaspoon of salt or mustard powder in a cup of warm water. Hold your cat's head, then force its mouth open with your thumb and index finger. Tilt its head back and pour the liquid as far back in the cat's mouth as possible. But *slowly!* The more slowly you pour, the less chance there is that your pet will gag or choke because of liquid in its windpipe.

Alternatively, use one teaspoon ordinary table salt. Force the cat's mouth open with your thumb and index finger, tilt its head, and throw salt as far back down the cat's throat as possible. If vomiting does not occur within ten minutes, repeat the process.

• *Never* attempt to induce vomiting if your cat is in shock or unconscious.

• For emergency treatment of acid poisoning, use one teaspoon bicarbonate of soda or four tablespoons of a mixture of a half pint of milk and one egg white.

• For emergency treatment of alkali poisoning, pour lemon juice or vinegar into the side of the cat's mouth to wash out the alkali.

• For emergency treatment of hyperactivity due to poisoning, give 2 mg of Chlor-Trimeton (half of a 4-mg tablet).

In all cases, rush the cat to a veterinarian.

## Shock Remedies

Shock may be caused by a variety of conditions—hemorrhage, severe injury, pain, poisoning, emotional trauma, fright—and in itself may be fatal. Symptoms are pale gums, cold body, rapid heartbeat, labored breathing, and coma.

• Keep the cat warm (wrapped in a blanket) and calm.

• If your pet is conscious, spill a teaspoon or so of warm, strong tea or brandy into its mouth. *Never give liquids if the cat is unconscious.* If it is unconscious, a drop of coffee or whiskey can be placed on its tongue, but smelling salts passed under its nose is generally more effective.

• A good antidote to keep on hand is a homemade remedy called Dr. Louis L. Vine's, a mixture of rock candy and brandy. Put four tablespoons of rock candy and three tablespoons of brandy in a covered jar. Let it stand for several days until it becomes syrupy. Keep tightly covered in a cool cabinet for emergency treatment.

## Good Policies for Swallowed Foreign Objects

There is no Heimlich maneuver for cats, but if yours swallows something that gets stuck in its throat, the best emergency tactic is to grasp your pet's hind legs, hoist, and shake gently. The foreign matter will usually be coughed up, but I advise taking your cat to the vet as soon as possible to be sure there's been no damage to its esophagus. If you don't know what the cat has swallowed, but you suspect it's something nonnutritive, follow the procedures above for inducing vomiting.

*Never* try to dig into your cat's throat with your fingers to dislodge a foreign object. If you can see the object in its mouth, fine. Otherwise, leave the digging to a professional.

When your cat is foreign-object-free, I'd advise giving its intestinal system a rest for at least twelve hours and then a soothing diet of pureed cooked lamb and rice, mixed with the contents of both a bee pollen and a 50-mg multiple B complex vitamin capsule, for at least the next two days.

## Bleeding

If you suspect internal bleeding, get your cat to the vet immediately. All you can do is watch for signs of shock and treat accordingly. If the bleeding is external, use ice packs, cold compresses, pressure, and tourniquets to control it until you can reach a doctor. When applying a tourniquet, remember to tie it above the wound and to loosen it every five minutes. Once your cat has returned home, I'd advise supplementing its meals with 100 mg of vitamin C and 50 mg of vitamin B complex or a quarter teaspoon of brewer's yeast until the wound has healed.

## How to Give Medication

*It's not fun, but when the job must be done,
you should know how to do it.*

Face it. Cats will never understand that when you give them medication you're only doing it for their own good. And even if they did understand, they still wouldn't enjoy the process. (Who does?) The giving and taking of medicine just isn't a fun activity for either party involved, but it needn't be a major battle, either.

### Pilling a Cat Painlessly

Coat the pill with butter, oil, or chicken fat, keeping it out of your cat's sight but within reach of your right hand. Get comfortable on a couch in front of the TV, and put the cat on your lap with its back toward you and its eyes facing the nightly news.

Begin loving, petting, and murmuring endearments, giving the cat time to forget any initial suspicion and relax. When you've got your pet purring, slyly stroke the sides of its face with the thumb and index finger of your left hand while surreptitiously picking up the pill with your right. Then, without flinching or breaking the mood, firmly force open the cat's mouth, tilting its head just slightly, pop the pill in (as far back on the center of the tongue as possible), quickly close the mouth, hold it (still murmuring softly), and gently stroke the cat's throat until it reflexively swallows. Keep petting and cooing for at least five more minutes, pretending that what has just happened was as much a surprise to you as it was for your cat.

Do not toss the animal to the floor the moment your mission is accomplished. Not only can this make future pill-giving a major problem, but your cat is likely to give you the cold shoulder for weeks.

### Pilling a Difficult Cat

Some cats cannot be fooled, and must be restrained in order to get medication into them. Wrap the animal in a towel from the neck down, making sure its paws are securely encased, then force open its mouth and proceed as described above.

### Cautions, Reminders, and Tips

• Always coat pills with some sort of oil, butter, or soft fat.
• If your cat begins to cough or gag, the pill might have gotten into its windpipe. Release its mouth immediately so the pill can be coughed up. If it isn't coughed up, you can help dislodge it by holding the cat upside down.
• If there's no way your cat will swallow a pill, turn the medication into a liquid and administer it with a plastic (not

glass) eyedropper. Fill the dropper with a solution of crushed pill mixed with a beaten raw egg yolk and a teaspoon or so of Karo syrup. Gently push the dropper between your pet's lips. If it tries to bite the dropper, the act will cause it to swallow. If this procedure doesn't work, you can try tilting the animal's head, just slightly, and administer the medicine slowly, making sure it does not enter the windpipe. If your cat begins to cough or gag, stop immediately.

• Another alternative for medicating zealous pill-protesters is to mix the crushed pill with an extremely appetizing, odor-masking food. Oil-packed sardines are your best bet—unless FUS is a problem, in which case sardines, high in magnesium, are a no-no. Forget trying to mix a crushed pill into your pet's regular food; a cat's nose knows.

## Questions and Answers About Getting Physical

### FISHY BUSINESS

*After I pet my cat, my hands smell sort of fishy. He's an indoor cat (domestic shorthair) and I can't imagine what's causing this. Is it normal for a cat to have body odor? Have you any idea what causes it and what I can do about it?*

No, it's not normal (a cat should not have a discernible body odor), but it does happen. Your pet's fishy smell might be caused by an excess of fish oil in his diet. Since there are sweat glands in a cat's paws, when your cat washes himself, the odor that's excreted is spread all over his fur. I'd suggest checking the oils that are in the foods he's eating or the supplements you might be giving, and switching to those that supply less odorous fats.

### FOREIGN AFFAIR

*My friend was told that her cat had "foreign body pneumonia." Is this communicable to other cats or humans?*

No. Foreign body pneumonia is caused by the ingestion of a substance or object that goes down the trachea instead of the esophagus and winds up in the lungs, causing an inflammation and/or infection, i.e., pneumonia. Though extremely difficult to cure, this type of pneumonia is not contagious among cats or transmittable to humans.

## HARRIED ABOUT HAIR BALLS

*My three-year-old Birman grooms herself freqently and is constantly distressed by hair balls. She's not what I would describe as a willing patient, and it's always a struggle to get medication down. Are there any foods she should be eating that would lessen her hair loss, and do you have any suggestions for easy hair-ball medicine administration?*

My first suggestion is that *you* begin grooming *her* more often, which should decrease some of the hair she's ingesting. My next is to be sure she's receiving high-BV protein and fat in her diet, and a good balanced fatty-acid supplement with vitamins. This, along with a humidifier in your home, should help minimize her shedding. As for administering hair-ball medicine, the simplest way is to buy a product such as Petromalt or Laxatone and put a fingerful on her nose or toes; she'll ingest it as she licks it off.

Be very careful about forcing hair-ball medication, as it's very easy for this to go down the wrong pipe (essentially the trachea) and cause problems, possibly foreign body pneumonia. Also be sure to give medicine between meals (not with, right before, or after) to prevent nutrient loss.

# *Getting Emotional*

❖❖❖❖❖❖❖

## Bad Behavior

*The more you know about a cat, the less trouble
you'll have with it.*

I've never met a bad cat, though quite a few brought to me are
described as such. Not, I must admit, without reason. They're
usually aggressive—biters, fighters, dauntless troublemakers
with unpleasant personalities and obnoxious habits. On occa-
sion they're spiteful introverts with mouselike machismo and
the charisma of soggy cornflakes.

The first idea I try to convey to the owner is that it is the
cat's *behavior,* not the cat itself, that is bad. What's the difference, you might ask (as many owners do). A big one. If the
cause of unsocial or abnormal behavior can be determined,
there's a chance of remedying it.

*A "Bad" Cat Is a Victim:* All "bad" cats are the unwitting
victims of circumstances beyond their control, but not neces-

sarily beyond that of their owners. Though it's true that certain undesirable traits are inherited, these can be controlled and even eliminated if the kitten is taken at four weeks and hand-raised. Unfortunately, this is not always possible. Therefore, I advise owners to find out as much as they can about a queen before picking a pet from her litter. To my mind, it's criminal for anyone to breed an overly nervous, aggressive, hyperactive, extremely timid, or otherwise genetically undesirable cat; yet, regrettably, people continue to do so.

Nevertheless, it's environment, not heredity, that molds most cats' behavior—and the person responsible for the ambience that surrounds a cat is you!

## Problems, Possible Causes, and Nutritional Remedies

*Feeding your cat for better behavior*

Many possible causes underlie behavioral problems in cats. Because some problems are often symptoms or side effects of injury or disease, *none* can be ignored. It's important, therefore, to consult a veterinarian who has examined your cat and knows its medical history before you make any of the dietary changes that I suggest here and throughout the book.

### Aggression

*Symptoms:* Biting, scratching, active hostility.

*Possible Cause:* Early subjection to abuse or indifference; impaired vision; brain tumor; inner-ear infection; any infection or pain; fear; environmental stress (a move, a new baby or pet in the household); domestic tension; maternal protectiveness; allergic reaction.

*For Your Information:* It is not normal for a cat to bite and scratch its owners, household members, or friends; sudden, unprovoked attacks should be brought to a veterinarian's attention. Train your cat when it's a kitten that biting is not allowed; you can do so by gently countering its nip with a quick finger-flick to the nose and a firm "no" while continuing to pet it. Foods rich in niacin (as well as all the B vitamins), tryptophan, and calcium are highly recommended for calming rambunctious little Rambos.

*Suggested Nutritional Remedy:* Discontinue feeding any supermarket/commercial food with artificial coloring or more than one preservative. (See chapter 10 for "Making the Food Transition" and my New-Life Diet.) Absolutely no soft-moist food should be offered.

• Add a quarter teaspoon of brewer's yeast and bran mix to food daily.

• One teaspoon chamomile tea three times daily, mixed with food or administered as described in chapter 7.

• Two tablespoons cottage cheese as a snack three times weekly.

• Replace two tablespoons regular food with two tablespoons finely chopped, cooked white-meat turkey (no skin) three to five times weekly.

• One quarter cup warm milk before bedtime.

### Shyness

*Symptoms:* Frightened, nervous, timid, hides.

*Possible Cause:* Insufficient physical contact with people or other animals; inherited nervousness; shock reaction to a frightening or painful experience (fight, explosion, sudden injury, surgery) or a narrow escape from one; early abandonment; central nervous system disorder; thyroid malfunction; gastrointestinal discomfort; overeating; any illness or pain.

*For Your Information:* Unless its shyness is genetically inherited, timidity in cats most commonly results from being raised in either a very noisy or a very cloistered environment, or having either extremely anxious or totally indifferent owners. Gastrointestinal upsets are common among shy and nervous cats, so you should make a special effort to supply easily digestible food and extra stress-fighting B vitamins.

*Suggested Nutritional Remedy:* If you are free feeding, leaving food down all day, discontinue immediately and switch your cat to two or three meals daily. No meal should be left down longer than thirty minutes. Feed meals in a quiet area, away from other pets or children.

• Add a half teaspoon brewer's yeast and contents of one bee pollen capsule to food daily.

• If you are not feeding an alternative/professional food, add a balanced fatty-acid supplement with zinc to meals three to six times weekly.

• Give 100 to 200 mg of vitamin C daily.

• Unless obesity is a problem, offer (from your hand) three small pieces of cheese or a few small tidbits of cooked chicken liver as a once-a-day treat.

• Provide large portions of TLC interactive play (such as blowing soap bubbles for your cat to chase), and regular daily petting or gentle grooming.

### Neurotic Behavior

*Symptoms:* Eating wool, fabrics, or feces; tail chewing.

*Possible Cause:* Lack of companionship or attention; dietary deficiency of vitamins, minerals, fiber, or digestive enzymes; worms; confinement; insufficient mental and physical stimulation; nonspecific illness or pain.

*For Your Information:* Wool and fabric eating, generally stemming from the frustrations of boredom, confinement, or inattention, is common among indoor cats whose diets are deficient primarily (though not exclusively) in fiber. Feces eating appears in cats with equivalent nutritional deficiencies, in the main caused by a perpetual cycling of intestinal parasites. Tail chewers are mostly feline versions of depressed, attention-deprived thumb suckers and nail biters. Owner enlightenment, in conjunction with nutrient supplementation, has proven enormously successful in eliminating these related problems.

*Suggested Nutritional Remedy:* If you are not feeding an alternative/professional food that includes beet pulp, whole grains, bran, or some other fiber, substitute one tablespoon of any of those—or canned green beans, lima beans, grated raw carrot, or peas—for an equal portion of your cat's regular food.

• Add a half teaspoon wheat germ and a quarter teaspoon brewer's yeast, once a day, to meals.

• Give 100 to 200 mg of vitamin C daily.

• Mix a quarter teaspoon catnip with a quarter cup tomato juice and offer it three to five times weekly. (If your cat is not elated by this treat, slip one to two teaspoons into the animal's food at least three times a week.)

• Provide an occasional large, cooked, nonsplintering shank bone for your cat to gnaw on.

• Serve ample helpings of TLC and activity daily.

### Forgetting Housebreaking

*Symptoms:* Spraying, ignoring the litter box, soiling floors and furniture.

*Possible Cause:* Hostility; urinary infection (cystitis); kidney disease; old age; illness; recuperation after surgery or illness; food dish and litter box too close to one another; spinal injury; head injury; emotional stress; unclean litter box.

*For Your Information:* Cats, under normal circumstances, are naturally fastidious and easily trained to use a litter box, but an infrequently cleaned litter box or one with scented litter can break their training. Urination in other household areas is often a symptom of cystitis (which causes painful, frequent voiding) or the result, after recovery, of having become habituated to not using the litter box. Geriatric cats frequently lose control of bladder and bowel function. Emotional stress, which can be caused by dietary as well as environmental changes, is generally the cause of voiding and defecating on furniture.

*Suggested Nutritional Remedy:* Put your cat on a low-magnesium diet (see chapter 11) as an FUS preventive or cure. Do not allow free feeding. Urine becomes more alkaline after eating, and all-day nibbling is not healthy for cats with FUS potential. Feed only quality high-BV-protein, low-ash (low-magnesium) food, with a long list of vitamins and minerals.

• Give 150 to 250 mg of vitamin C and 50 to 75 mg of vitamin B complex daily.

• Mix one to two teaspoons tomato juice into canned food three to five times weekly.

• Supply plenty of water. Hard water contains magnesium, so I'd suggest you provide noncarbonated bottled water at room temperature and keep it fresh daily.

• Keep the food dish and the litter box in separate areas. (You wouldn't want to dine in your bathroom, would you?)

• Provide attention and activity (particularly for toms and altered males) to prevent boredom and frustration, which are often the cause of indoor spraying.

## Questions and Answers About Getting Emotional

### MAINE COON MANIAC

*I have a large four-year-old Maine coon who has turned into a destructive maniac. His name is Jack, and I've taken to calling him Jack the Ripper because of the way he's clawed up the house. My couch and draperies are ruined, but I'm not buying new ones until I can get Jack under control. He has a scratching post and behaves when I'm around, but when I go to work, so does he—on everything. I'd hate to have him declawed, but I don't know what else to do. Help!*

At this point, I wouldn't advise declawing. Jack's scratching instinct sounds firmly ingrained, and I've seen declawed cats develop pad calluses that worked as well as nails insofar as destroying furniture. Catching him in the act and shouting a blaring "no" while swatting a newspaper against your hand might help, but you have to be consistent. Whenever he stops, reward him with a wealth of affection, and then direct him toward the scratching post. (Coating it with a catnip spray could make it more appealing.)

Since you indicate that this behavior is recent, some physical or environmental change appears to be responsible. My advice is to alleviate some of the stress by increasing Jack's intake of B vitamins. I'd suggest adding the contents of a balanced 50-mg B complex capsule, a quarter teaspoon of brewer's yeast, and one to two teaspoons of chamomile tea to his daily meals. Keep him off any foods that contain artificial colorings or more than one preservative. When you're at home, try to distract him with play, such as blowing bubbles or letting a shoelace trail behind your foot so that he'll follow it around and have your company, too. It's probably also worth purchasing a nonstaining cat repellent spray (available at pet stores) for your couch and draperies . . . just to be on the safe side.

## A PICA PAIR

*I have two cats that eat litter box filler and sometimes eat or lick the cement on the sidewalk. They drink milk every day and eat a variety of canned and dry cat foods. I also give them a Nu-tri Cal vitamin at least two or three times a week. I can't figure out what's missing in their diet or why they're doing this.*

Your cats are evidencing behavior known as pica, an abnormal craving for unnatural foods. The primary cause is probably a nutritional deficiency, though not necessarily in both cats. It's not uncommon for one cat to mimic pica behavior in another. Nonetheless, I'd suggest a change in diet and some behavior-modification tactics for both.

Feed a quality alternative food (see chapter 4) of high caloric density so your cats will be able to get optimum nutrition from minimum portions. Feed *only* that food, twice daily, for at least two weeks. Do not add any supplements. These could interfere with the availability of the alternative food's nutrients, which are specifically balanced for maximum utilization. During these two weeks, use a different brand of litter, and keep the cats away from the cement.

At the end of the two weeks, spray the cement with a cat repellent and reintroduce your pets to the area. Even if the pica behavior is remembered, it's unlikely that either of your cats will be eager to resume the old habit.

## FOILING A FECES EATER

*I've changed my cat's diet. I change her litter box daily. I give her more attention than I do my husband, and yet she's still eating her feces. I can't think of a solution, nor can my vet, and since I never had any faith in Sherlock Holmes, I'm hoping you'll be able to come up with an answer.*

Why, it's excrementary, my dear. (I couldn't resist that.) There are actually several solutions. MSG or a prescription product called Forbid (which your vet should have) can be added to your cat's food, causing no harm to your pet, but making her feces extremely distasteful. Or you can pour a hot-pepper sauce such as Tabasco on her stools, which ought to undevelop her taste for them in short order.

# Getting Territorial

❖❀❖❀❖❀❖❀

## The Indoor Cat

*Easily satisfied, easily cared for, its special needs can be too easily ignored.*

Some cats are more suited than others to the indoor life (see chapter 6), but virtually all can become conditioned to it. The conditioning process is not difficult, provided you understand that cats are inherently territorial, are creatures of habit, have unique nutritional needs, and that their natural instincts don't disappear just because they've been raised on canned prey in a world of wall-to-wall carpeting.

*Pitfalls of Raising an Indoor Cat:* The needs of indoor cats are often misunderstood by well-meaning owners who tend to lavish food on their pets as a demonstration of affection, unknowingly defeating their purpose by setting up the animals they love for a major fall from health. With limited space comes limited activity. Limited activity plus unlimited calories adds on pounds and sums up to obesity (see chapter 11), decreasing the cat's life expectancy and increasing its chances for an unpleasant assortment of ailments.

Another common pitfall is allowing the cat to dictate its own diet ("Oh, Mommy's poor baby's been alone all day so I'll give her anything she wants"), which usually winds up being a single food (or type of food) that excludes all others. You thus not only create a finicky eater—that cute term pet food companies exploit to sell foods that create more finicky eaters—but a powerful food addiction. So powerful is this addiction that if at any future time a prescription diet becomes a life-or-death necessity, the cat might only be capable of opting for the second choice.

*Feeding for Close Quarters:* The best foods for any cat, providing it has no specially prescribed dietary restrictions, are, as far as I'm concerned, those with the highest protein/fat digestibility and utilization. (See chapter 4.) These foods not only supply optimal nutrition but produce fewer and less odorous stools, which, let's face it, is a definite plus for anyone living with a cat in a small apartment.

*Health Memos:* Because they are deprived of seasonal natural light and temperature cycles, which influence shedding, most indoor cats will shed year-round. They are therefore more prone to hair balls and likely to need hair-ball medication at least once or twice a week. Grooming is necessary, even for shorthairs, since their environment does not provide the tall-grass natural brushing available to outdoor cats.

Offer your indoor cat opportunities for as much exercise play as possible. If you're too busy to interact with your pet, a paper bag (for pouncing on, crawling in and out of, batting around) or rubber ball can keep an indoor cat amused and active for quite a while.

Be sure its diet includes ample vitamin D, since indoor cats are denied the benefit of sunlight's ultraviolet rays, which produce the vitamin naturally in outdoor animals.

## The Outdoor Cat

*The more territory it roams, the greater
its health hazards.*

An outdoor cat is not necessarily one who *lives* outdoors, but
(at least for the purposes of this book) one who has the
freedom and opportunity to spend a substantial amount of
unsupervised time outside the confines of its home. Whether
you put your cat out at night or let it in then, the hours your
pet spends on its own—and the way that it spends them—
definitely affect its physical and emotional well-being.

*Dangerous Assumptions About Outdoor Cats:* Because felines
are natural outdoor survivalists, many owners assume that
their cat will instinctively take care of itself, as well as cure its
own ailments, if allowed enough time outside. Well, from my
veterinary experience, let me tell you that this just ain't so.
Simply because you've seen your cat eat grass to cough up a
hair ball or unload its stomach doesn't prove anything more
than its need for better grooming and more dietary supervision.

Once a cat is outdoors, it's going to follow its instincts, and
these are what most often lead to trouble. Carnivorous and
predatory, a cat, no matter what you feed it, will rarely pass up
the chance to bring down an unwary bird or rodent. Even if
that prey is not eaten, but just brought to your door with a
proud "meow," it's highly unlikely that your cat won't—if it
hasn't already—eventually want a taste of its catch and invaria-
bly ingest more than desired. In two words: internal parasites;
in one: worms.

Cats with well-fortified immune systems are more resistant
to the debilitating effects of worms (see chapter 11), which can
be contracted in numerous ways. This is particularly true of
outdoor felines, who are also more susceptible to contagious
viral and bacterial infections, because of the increased possibility of contact with sick strays and access to contaminated
food or water.

*Health Memos:* If your pet is a four-footed nature lover, I strongly recommend feeding a daily diet of high-BV protein, vitamin-enriched alternative food (see chapter 4), supplemented with a quarter teaspoon of brewer's yeast and 50 to 75 mg of vitamin C.

Before letting a kitten or cat outside, be sure it has received all essential inoculations (distemper, rhino-tracheitis, pneumonitis, calici-virus, rabies) and any required annual booster shots.

## The Multi-Cat Home

*When there's more than one, don't double the problems, double the fun.*

Cats, by nature, are solitary animals, but, by golly, they can enjoy company. Not all cats, of course, and not all the time . . . and not always the companions we choose for them. . . . Nonetheless, as every cat lover knows, once you're hooked on one, there will usually be another (if not more) in your future—and your home—a lot sooner than you think.

*Coping Simplified:* When you're dealing with cats, proper introductions have nothing to do with etiquette and everything to do with establishing peace (or at least détente) and keeping your sanity intact.

If the new arrival is a kitten, speak softly, handle gently, and put it in a quiet room away from your resident pet (and children). Provide fresh water, food, a litter pan, and a soft resting place, and allow the kitten to investigate its new surroundings at its own pace. Your resident pet will be curious about the intruder, but for the first few days do not leave them alone together. Hostility is natural and can be hazardous to a kitten's health. The two will soon establish a relationship.Giving your older cat some extra affection during this period will help make that relationship a friendlier one.

If you bring in an adult cat, plan on postponing pet introductions for at least five days. This newcomer will usually be heavily stressed and behaviorally unpredictable. It needs readjustment time in an off-limits living space of its own in order to feel secure and come to trust you. Patience in this situation is not just a virtue, it's a necessity for communal cat comfort.

*Health Memos:* Extra attention and B vitamins (either brewer's yeast or 50 to 75 mg of B complex) should be given to the new cat as well as your resident pet during this period and for at least two weeks after they've been introduced.

Each cat should have its own feeding dish. If either cat begins vomiting after meals, which is often caused by competitive eating (rapid gobbling of food), feed them in different areas or at different times.

Be sure any new cat you bring home has been fully inoculated for communicable diseases before introducing it to your resident pets.

## When Cats Live with Other Animals

*How to keep purrr-fect harmony in
an interspecies household*

Whether a cat shares its home with dogs, hamsters, birds, snakes, guinea pigs, parakeets, or kids, it still needs a place to call its own and will usually find and claim it all by itself. The myth that dogs and cats are natural adversaries is just that: a myth. In domestic situations animals aren't born enemies, they're made. And once you realize that any multi-pet home can run as smoothly as Noah's ark with a little common sense, consistent rules, and the word "no," you've got it all made.

*Avoiding Mealtime Mayhem:* Food is really the only problem, especially if any of your pets happen to be natural feline fare. A new cat entering a home that has a resident bird or gerbil shouldn't be expected to know that these are its neighbors and not its larder. But it can learn. It's easy enough to teach a kitten by squirting it with a toy water pistol any time it even approaches those animals' cages, but older cats can be more difficult to dissuade. For them, I'd suggest keeping your smaller, ingestible pets secured in rooms the cat is *never* allowed to enter. And I do mean never. Even the sweetest, gentlest cat in the world is capable of taking a lethal swipe at a small caged creature, so boundaries must be firmly established and precautions taken.

As for regular feeding of cats and dogs in the same household, the important idea to remember is that they need separate dining areas or different eating times. Most dogs adore cat food, and since they're also prone to competitive eating, they often scarf down their own meal and then go for the cat's. If you're unaware of this, you may find your cat inexplicably losing weight, always appearing hungry, and possibly convince yourself (and even your vet) that there's a medical problem, when in fact it's a canine one. On the other hand, cats will often eat dog food, which is deficient in taurine (essential for felines) and become too full to eat their own nutritious dinners.

*Health Memos:* Supervise dog and cat mealtimes, and do not leave food down all day for either animal.

Never serve more than one animal from the same feeding dish.

Add brewer's yeast to both the cat's and dog's food daily. A little stress prevention never hurts.

If one animal has worms, the other should be checked for them, since they are commonly transmitted between cats and dogs.

Keep track of inoculations and yearly booster shots. Even if your cat doesn't leave the house, your dog most likely does and can bring home big trouble.

Conjunctivitis, an inflammation of the tissues surrounding the eye, can be transmitted from dog to cat and vice versa. Though not all types of conjunctivitis are contagious, it's best to quarantine the afflicted pet until you get an okay from your vet.

## Changing Your Cat's Environment

*When a cat is moved from one environment to another,
a formerly right diet might turn out to be all wrong.*

A move is never easy for anyone, but it's especially difficult for
cats. Whether you're taking your pet south for the winter or
bringing it up north to a friend, there are emotional and
nutritional considerations that should be kept in mind.

*Right Moves:* When your cat arrives at its new home, do not
expect it to behave as usual. This is all new territory for the
animal, unfamiliar turf, and no matter how lovely the new
environment, your cat is not going to be thrilled.

If you're used to letting your pet outdoors, do not do so
unless there is a fenced-in area or you walk it on a leash for at
least two weeks. As remarkable as cats are for finding their way
home, it will take awhile for them to get used to a new one.
And if they don't like the new home, they just might try to
hightail it back to their old one.

If you're leaving your cat with a friend, bring along some of
your pet's familiar things (toys, bed, feeding dish), and be sure
to have your friend keep to the animal's regular feeding schedule and diet. Adding 50 to 75 mg of B complex to the food will
help reduce stress, and replacing a fourth of the cat's first few
meals with a favorite treat meat or protein will soften the blow
of staying with a stranger.

Now, if the move is to another climate—from sunny south-
ern California to Canada, for example—you're going to have to
change the cat's diet. Cats use a certain amount of fat and
calories for thermoregulation of body temperature. If your pet
has been enjoying the warmth in L.A., sleeping out in the sun
and getting plenty of vitamin D, the animal's caloric and
vitamin needs will be increased in a colder climate. And if
you're headed the other way, the reverse will be true. In either
case, you should make the diet changes slowly, keeping the cat

indoors and allowing its body time to ease into warming up or cooling down.

*Health Memos:* For cold climates, I'd advise adding a balanced fatty-acid supplement to the cat's food daily for at least two to three weeks, along with a quarter teaspoon of brewer's yeast, 100 to 200 mg of vitamin C, and 50 to 75 mg of balanced vitamin B complex. Make sure water in the feeding area does not become too cold.

For warm climates, increase the cat's intake of liquids. If your pet doesn't like the taste of the new water, stock up on bottled noncarbonated water and offer that, at least until your pet gets used to the regular water. I've found that letting a faucet drip slowly often gets even water-loathing cats to drink. Adding one to two teaspoons of tomato juice to canned food is also a good idea. Feed smaller portions of food for the first two weeks, along with a quarter teaspoon of brewer's yeast, 100 to 200 mg of vitamin C, and 50 to 75 mg of balanced vitamin B complex.

## Traveling with Your Cat

*It can be fun for both of you—and you and your feline friend can go a lot more places than you think.*

Cats are really great traveling companions and enjoy it, if you give them the chance. Obviously, if the only time you've ever taken your cat in the car is for a trip to the vet, the animal is not going to be enthusiastic about a motoring trip. Cats can easily adjust to motion, but the trick is getting them to enjoy it. Start by taking your cat with you in the car for a short (five-minute) drive around the block. (I'd advise doing this *before* or at least two hours *after* the animal has eaten.) Then, every day gradually increase the length of travel time. Don't put the cat in a carrying case or box during these training rides. Give your pet a chance to adjust. It might take a few trips, but you'll be surprised how quickly a cat can learn to find a comfortable spot and settle down.

## Travel Tips and Cautions

• Never leave your cat in a locked car with no ventilation. Always leave a window slightly open; make sure that the opening is not large enough for the cat to squeeze through.

• Bring water and dish along for long rides, though don't give it to the animal within two hours of departure unless it's very hot.

• Never let your cat out of the car in a strange area unless the animal is on a leash.

• When you have to use a pet carrier (on buses, trains, planes, in taxis), make sure that the container is sturdy, allows visibility, is large enough for comfort with perhaps a toy or blanket, and that you've gotten your pet used to it before the trip. I highly recommend a soft, heavy-duty nylon carrier. They look like shoulder bags and come with screen windows, roll-down flaps, and a double-zippered top; and cats love being able to feel your closeness when carried in them. (Le Pet Bag, manufactured by Doggiduds Inc., New York, is the best I've found.)

• Be sure your pet wears a collar with an identification tag.

• Don't feed your cat for several hours before traveling.

• Take along enough dry food for at least two meals.

• Exercise your pet before the journey.

• Tryptophan, a natural relaxant, can be given in pediatric dosage before departure, and every six hours if necessary. If you are flying, consult your vet aboout the advisability of a sedative.

• Supplement food during travel with 50 to 75 mg of B complex and 100 to 200 mg of vitamin C.

• Be sure your cat has had all its inoculations and a certificate of health from your vet (the document is required in many states and all foreign countries). If you are traveling to a foreign country, your pet's certificate of health must be validated by the federal veterinarian for your state.

• Don't take your pet traveling if it's pregnant, sick, recuperating from illness, hyperactive, nervous, feeble, or in heat.

## Questions and Answers About Getting Territorial

### A Puzzlement

*My two-year-old cat, Flick-Flack, a British shorthair, is in good health and good condition, but always has an itch on the sides of his head. I don't see any redness or hair loss, but he's constantly rubbing the sides of his forehead against the couch, my legs, even his food dish. He doesn't go outside, and I have no other pets. At this point, it has me stratching my own head trying to figure out what's causing this. Can you?*

It sounds as if he's simply marking his favorite objects. A cat has a gland on both sides of its forehead (the temporal gland) and uses this to leave its scent on things and people it likes. Two cats will often rub heads, leaving their scents on each other to confirm friendship, sort of like becoming blood brothres. Don't worry about Flick-Flack. He's not itchy, he's just in love.

# PART FOUR

# Dr. Jane's New-Life Nutrition Plan

❖✿❖❀❖✿❖

# Thirty Days to a Healthier Cat

❖❀❖❀❖❀❖

## Making the Food Transition

*How to put your cat on the path to optimal health*

Before we begin, there's one phrase you must put out of your mind: *"But my cat will only eat ——,"* because my response to this is "Nonsense!" Your cat knows who provides its food, and it will eventually eat what you feed it. Even if you've made the mistake of offering your pet options and unwittingly created a gustatorial dictator, food addictions, difficult as they appear to be, are not impossible to break. The key is simply knowing how to go about it and caring enough for your pet to stick to the new routine.

*Go Slow for Success:* Though some cats will eat a new food even if it's not as tasty as their usual food just for the novelty of it, most will want to revert back to their more palatable, familiar fare in a few days. This can be frustrating, and undermine your efforts to succeed at making dietary changes. (Once cats know they can have their own way food-wise, they've got you under their paws—and know it.)

The best way to make a food transition is to do it gradually, slowly—over a period of days—mixing increasing amounts of new food with decreasing portions of the old. For hard-core finicky eaters, start by removing just one teaspoon of the old food and replacing it with an equivalent amount of the new. Once the cat accepts this, increase the switch to two teaspoons and so on, until the conversion is complete. But be patient. Too much too soon can put the cat on to your plan and off the new food for months.

## Getting Your Cat into Dry Food

*Don't let your cat's teeth be without it.*

If your cat's a confirmed canned-food eater, chances are it's going to respond less than enthusiastically to a surprise meal of dry food. But since dry food is essential to good dental health, the sooner you accustom your cat to eating it on a regular basis (at least three to five times a week), the better.

Moistening dry food defeats its tartar-removing and gum-exercising purposes. But if your cat's not used to crunching food, softening the animal's introduction to it is advised. Unless we're dealing with kittens (see chapter 5), which we're not in this section, the best way to get a non-dry-food eater started is to mix a teaspoon of dry food (removing an equivalent amount of canned) with the cat's regular fare. This will moisten the dry just enough to give your pet a chance to get used to a new texture (mouth feel) without causing the cat culinary trauma or eliciting a strong negative reaction, such as punting its food dish across the floor.

If you know that your cat is extremely finicky and texture-oriented, you might want to ensure the success of this first foray into dry by coating the teaspoon of added food with some melted butter or bacon grease, or warming the dry food to enhance its flavor.

When your cat begins accepting the new item, increase the amount with each meal (decreasing the equivalent amount of canned food) until your pet is eating a completely dry meal. Once it is doing so, feed *only* dry food for at least three days in a row. Don't waver from this! If your cat discovers that a plaintive "meow" will set you running for the can opener, you're sunk, and your pet will miss out on a very important factor in dental health.

After your cat has become accustomed to dry food, you can alternate between canned and dry meals, making sure, though, that you feed dry at least three to five times weekly.

## Four Weeks to a Fitter Feline: The New-Life Diet for Your Cat

*How to revitalize and maximize your cat's health, beauty, and disease resistance within thirty days*

My New-Life Diet is designed for average adult cats (approximately eight pounds) with no special medical problems. (For those, see the special diets in chapter 11.) If your cat is much larger or smaller, adjust food quantities according to the basic calorie needs given in chapter 2.

I've formulated this program to promote optimal health for all cats through a simple, nutritionally balanced feeding regimen. If adhered to, my New-Life Diet can not only strengthen your pet's immune system and increase vitality but also produce *visible* physical and behavioral improvements within two to four weeks.

CAUTION: If your cat is currently on medication, being treated for illness, taking supplements, on any prescription food, or hasn't had a professional checkup within the last year, consult your veterinarian before making any changes in your pet's diet.

*Make no mistake:* The Sunday treat meals are meant to be just once-a-week indulgences. They are optional, flexible, interchangeable with other treat recipes or your cat's favorite food, and can be served on whatever day you choose. *But only once a week!*

## New-Life Diet Restrictions

- No soft-moist foods
- No supermarket/commercial or generic cat foods
- No self-feeding (access to food at all times) unless an emergency situation arises and you have no other recourse
- No meal left down for more than twenty to thirty minutes
- No table scraps other than those approved for use in special or treat meals
- No *raw* meat, fish, or organ meats

## The New-Life Shopping List

**Dry Food** (any of the following)
Iams
Science Diet/Feline Maintenance (Hill's)
Super Stars (Cornucopia)
Hi-Tor (Triumph)
Tamiami (Beatrice)
Lick Your Chops

**Canned Food** (any of the following)
Feline Maintenance (Hill's)
Tamiami (Beatrice)
Triumph (Triumph)
Cornucopia (Cornucopia)
Lick Your Chops

**Frozen Cat Food**—optional, but recommended (any of the following)
Showbound's Total Feline (Champion Foods)
Showbound's Beef, Liver, Chicken, etc. (Champion Foods)
Jespy

**Sundries**
• A balanced fatty-acid supplement with linoleic, linolenic, and arachidonic acids, as well as vitamins A, $B_6$, and E, biotin, and zinc (available at pet, feed, and health food stores as well as from veterinarians and breeders)
• Bee pollen capsules (available at health food stores, pet stores, pharmacies, and wherever vitamins are sold)
• Brewer's yeast (available wherever vitamins are sold)
• Brewer's yeast and bran mix (available wherever vitamins are sold)
• Wheat germ oil (available wherever vitamins are sold)
• Wheat germ (available at supermarkets and wherever vitamins are sold)
• Catnip (available at pet and health food stores)
• Freeze-dried beef, liver, or fish treats (available at pet and feed stores)
• Calcium tablets, 50 mg (available wherever vitamins are sold)

## A Special Word About Water

Fresh water—never ice cold or warm—must be available to your cat at all times. If you live in an area where there is hard water (high in magnesium) or use a home water softener (which adds sodium), I'd recommend you get bottled noncarbonated water for your cat's health and your own.

## Exercises for Feline Fitness

No health program (for cats or people) can be successful without exercise. For this reason, it's important to devote twenty minutes—ideally, ten minutes in the morning and ten in the evening—to playing with your cat. Do this before, between, or at least an hour after the cat has eaten. If your weekday schedule does not permit a morning cat workout, plan an evening exercise break. Even if your own idea of a workout is a nice brisk sit, you can shape up your pet emotionally and physically in such ways as these:

• Relax in a chair and blow soap bubbles, which cats love to leap for and pop.

• Trail a piece of string or a shoelace behind you that the cat can pursue.

• Roll a catnip-filled toy that your pet can bat back and forth to you.

• Call your pet when you're in another room and then give it a good, loving stroking when it comes.

You will find that these simple combinations of attention, affection, and activity in conjunction with my New-Life Diet will accelerate and undeniably demonstrate the rewards of optimal feline fitness.

## The New-Life Menu Plan

### THE FIRST WEEK

*Monday*

A.M.  ¼ cup dry. If cat isn't used to dry food, follow procedure described above in "Getting Your Cat into Dry Food."

P.M.  ½ cup canned. If cat is hooked on supermarket/commercial food, follow procedure described above in "Making the Food Transition."

SNACK 2 or 3 *dice-size* pieces of Cheddar, American, or Muenster cheese. Can be given midafternoon or evening, not both.

*Tuesday*

A.M. ½ cup canned. If left over and refrigerated from previous day, bring to room temperature by adding ½ teaspoon boiling water or broth.

P.M. ½ cup canned. Bring to room temperature by adding ½ teaspoon boiling water or broth.

SNACK 3 cooked (fresh or canned) string beans dipped in melted butter or soft fat. Can be given midafternoon or evening, not both.

*Wednesday*

A.M. ¼ cup dry

P.M. ¼ cup dry with 1 raw egg yolk (no white) or 2 tablespoons cottage cheese or yogurt

SNACK 2 sardines (if FUS is not a problem), or 1 *small* cooked chicken liver chopped in bite-size pieces. Can be given midafternoon or evening, not both.

*Thursday*

A.M. ½ cup canned

P.M. ½ cup canned with ¼ cup cooked fish (boneless flounder, haddock, sole) or chicken, contents of 1 bee pollen capsule, and ½ teaspoon boiling water. Mix well and be sure food is at room temperature.

SNACK 2 tablespoons canned lima beans, green beans, or peas. Can be given midafternoon or evening, not both.

*Friday*

A.M. ¼ cup dry

P.M.     1 teaspoon less than ½ cup canned; add 1 teaspoon
         buttered, cooked, and chopped canned green
         beans, peas, or raw grated carrot.

SNACK    2 or 3 *dice-size* pieces of Cheddar, American, or
         Muenster cheese. Can be given midafternoon or
         evening, not both.

### Saturday
A.M.     ¼ cup dry
P.M.     3 ounces frozen complete cat food or ½ cup canned
SNACK    3 small (rounded-teaspoon-size) pieces of can-
         taloupe, avocado, or grapes. Can be given mid-
         afternoon and evening.

### Sunday
A.M.     ## COTTAGE 'N' EGG BRUNCH

1 egg
½ teaspoon butter
1 tablespoon creamed cottage cheese
1 eggshell, cooked and finely ground, or 1 pulverized
    50-mg calcium tablet
¼ teaspoon wheat germ

Scramble egg in butter over low flame, slowly
mixing in cottage cheese and eggshell (or calcium).
As soon as egg white is cooked, remove from stove.
Put mixture in cat's dish and stir in wheat germ. Be
sure to allow meal to cool before serving.

P.M.     ¼ cup dry
SNACK    2 or 3 dried liver treats. Can be given midafternoon
         or evening, not both.

### THE SECOND WEEK

### Monday
A.M.     ¼ cup dry
P.M.     3 ounces frozen complete cat food, or ½ cup canned

SNACK 2 tablespoons yogurt with or without ¼ teaspoon catnip, or ¼ cup skim milk. Can be given mid-afternoon or evening, not both.

### Tuesday
A.M. ½ cup canned

P.M. 3 ounces canned with 1 ounce cooked and finely chopped chicken, turkey, or fish (boneless sole, bluefish, haddock). Add ½ teaspoon boiling water or broth to bring food to room temperature if necessary.

SNACK 2 tablespoons canned lima beans, green beans, or peas, or 3 cooked asparagus spears. Can be given midafternoon or evening, not both.

### Wednesday
A.M. ¼ cup dry

P.M. ½ cup canned with ¼ teaspoon wheat germ, contents of 1 bee pollen capule, and ½ teaspoon boiling water or broth to bring to room temperature if necessary

SNACK 2 or 3 dried beef treats. Can be given midafternoon or evening, not both.

### Thursday
A.M. ¼ cup dry with 1 raw egg yolk or 1 whole parboiled egg

P.M. ½ cup canned

SNACK 3 cooked (fresh or canned) string beans dipped in melted butter or soft fat. Can be given midafternoon or evening, not both.

### Friday
A.M. ½ cup canned with ½ teaspoon boiling water or broth to bring to room temperature if necessary

P.M. ½ cup canned with ¼ cup dry

SNACK     2 or 3 pitted green olives with or without pimiento. Can be given midafternoon and evening.

*Saturday*

A.M.      ¼ cup dry with 2 tablespoons skim milk, cottage cheese, or yogurt

P.M.      3 ounces complete frozen cat food or ½ cup canned

SNACK     2 tablespoons canned lima beans, green beans, or peas, or 3 cooked asparagus spears. Can be given midafternoon and evening.

*Sunday*

A.M.      ¼ cup dry

P.M.      **SEAFOOD SPECIAL SUNDAY TREAT**

½ cup drained and finely chopped canned clams
2 tablespoons creamed cottage cheese
½ teaspoon soybean, peanut, or corn oil
⅛ teaspoon brewer's yeast
1 eggshell, cooked and finely ground, or 1 pulverized 50-mg calcium tablet
1 teaspoon finely grated carrot

Combine all ingredients, mixing well. Serve with ¼ teaspoon melted butter dribbled on top.

SNACK     2 or 3 dried beef or liver treats. Can be given midafternoon or evening, not both.

### THE THIRD WEEK

*Monday*

A.M.      ¼ cup dry

P.M.      ½ cup canned

SNACK     2 sardines (unless FUS is a problem), or 1 *small* cooked chicken liver chopped in bite-size pieces. Can be given midafternoon or evening, not both.

*Tuesday*

A.M.    ½ cup canned with ½ teaspoon boiling water or broth to bring it to room temperature if necessary

P.M.    3 ounces canned mixed with 1 ounce cooked chicken or turkey, finely chopped, 1 cooked green bean, finely chopped, and ½ teaspoon boiling water or broth to bring to room temperature if necessary

SNACK   3 pitted green olives with or without pimiento. Can be given midafternoon and evening.

*Wednesday*

A.M.    ¼ cup dry

P.M.    ¼ cup dry with 1 raw egg yolk or 1 whole parboiled egg

SNACK   2 tablespoons cooked and boned herring or white-fish. Can be given midafternoon or evening, not both.

*Thursday*

A.M.    ½ cup canned

P.M.    3 ounces canned mixed with 1 teaspoon buttered, cooked, and chopped canned peas or lima beans and ½ teaspoon boiling water or broth to bring food to room temperature if necessary

SNACK   2 or 3 *dice-size* pieces of Cheddar, American, or Muenster cheese. Can be given midafternoon or evening, not both.

*Friday*

A.M.    ¼ cup dry

P.M.    ½ cup canned mixed with ⅛ teaspoon brewer's yeast and bran mix and ½ teaspoon boiling water or broth to bring to room temperature if necessary

SNACK   3 small (rounded-teaspoon-size) pieces of cantaloupe, avocado, or grapes. Can be given midafternoon and evening.

*Saturday*
A.M.   ¼ cup dry
P.M.   3½ ounces frozen complete cat dinner, or ½ cup
canned
SNACK   2 tablespoons yogurt or cottage cheese with or without ¼ teaspoon catnip. Can be given midafternoon or evening, not both.

*Sunday*
A.M.   **BONANZA BRUNCH**

1 egg
½ teaspoon butter or bacon grease
1 eggshell, cooked and finely ground, or 1 pulverized
50-mg calcium tablet
½ ounce cream cheese, softened and cubed
¼ teaspoon wheat germ

Beat egg and scramble over low flame in butter or
bacon grease. Add the ground cooked eggshell (or
calcium) and cubed cream cheese. Remove from
flame as soon as cheese melts. (Egg should be soft
and creamy.) Mix in wheat germ. Serve at room
temperature, not hot.

P.M.   ½ cup canned
SNACK   2 tablespoons canned lima beans, green beans, or
peas, or 3 cooked asparagus spears. Can be given
midafternoon or evening, not both.

## THE FOURTH WEEK

*Monday*
A.M.     ¼ cup dry with ⅛ teaspoon balanced fatty acid
P.M.     ½ cup canned mixed with ¼ teaspoon brewer's yeast and bran mix and ½ teaspoon boiling water or broth to bring to room temperature if necessary
SNACK   2 or 3 dried fish or liver treats. Can be given mid-afternoon or evening, not both.

*Tuesday*
A.M.     ¼ cup dry
P.M.     ½ cup canned
SNACK   2 or 3 *dice-size* pieces of your cat's favorite cheese. Can be given midafternoon or evening, not both.

*Wednesday*
A.M.     ¼ cup dry with 1 raw egg yolk or 1 whole parboiled egg
P.M.     ½ cup canned
SNACK   2 tablespoons canned lima beans, green beans, or peas, or 3 cooked asparagus spears. Can be given midafternoon and evening.

*Thursday*
A.M.     ¼ cup dry
P.M.     3 ounces canned mixed with 1 ounce chopped cooked turkey, lamb, chicken, or boneless fish and ½ teaspoon boiling water or broth to bring to room temperature if necessary
SNACK   3 pitted green olives, with or without pimiento. Can be given midafternoon and evening.

*Friday*

A.M.     ¼ cup dry

P.M.     ½ cup canned with ½ teaspoon boiling water or broth to bring to room temperature if necessary

SNACK   2 sardines (if FUS is not a problem), or 1 *small* cooked chicken liver chopped in bite-size pieces

*Saturday*

A.M.     ¼ cup dry

P.M.     3½ ounces frozen complete cat food, or ½ cup canned

SNACK   2 tablespoons yogurt or cottage cheese mixed with ⅛ teaspoon wheat germ. Can be given midafternoon or evening, not both.

*Sunday*

A.M.     ¼ cup dry

P.M.     **DR. JANE'S STEAK AND KIDNEY CASSEROYAL**

2 ounces ground chuck or hamburger beef
1 ounce lamb or beef kidneys, finely chopped
1 French-style green bean, cut into 8 pieces
1 eggshell, cooked and finely ground, or 1 pulverized 50-mg calcium tablet
½ teaspoon soybean, peanut, or corn oil
1 tablespoon oatmeal

Preheat oven to 350° F. Combine ingredients and mix well in small casserole dish. Cover and bake for 20 to 30 minutes. Allow to cool before serving in cat's own food dish.

SNACK   Your pet's choice. Can be given midafternoon and evening.

## More New-Life Brunch and Dinner Treat Recipes

*A selection of healthy meals with feline taste appeal for occasional (no more than once a week) special occasions*

### CAESAR SALAD FOR YOUR FELINE

1 large lettuce leaf (not chicory), finely shredded
¼ teaspoon finely diced celery
1 hard-boiled egg, chopped
¼ cup diced cooked chicken, turkey, and/or roast beef
1 tablespoon diced canned string beans, peas, or lima beans
1–2 pitted green olives with or without pimiento
⅛ teaspoon wheat germ
1 teaspoon shredded Cheddar cheese (or cat's favorite)
*Dressing:*
2 tablespoons oil from "people" tuna fish with pinch of garlic powder
or
2–3 tablespoons gravy from favorite canned food (mixed with water if necessary)

Toss ingredients with dressing and put in cat's feeding dish. Top with any of the following: 1 chopped anchovy, 1 chopped boneless sardine, or ½ slice of cooked, crumbled bacon.

### SHRIMP 'N' CHEESE 'N' MORE

2–3 cooked baby shrimp, chopped
1 tablespoon creamed cottage cheese
1 tablespoon finely diced cooked chicken or turkey with skin
⅛ teaspoon brewer's yeast
1 eggshell, cooked and finely ground, or 1 pulverized 50-mg calcium tablet
½ teaspoon melted butter or chicken fat

Combine shrimp, cottage cheese, chicken or turkey, brewer's yeast, and eggshell (or calcium). Put in feeding dish and dribble melted butter or chicken fat on top before serving.

## BEEFY CHEESEBURGER BLITZ

¼ cup fatty hamburger beef
1 tablespoon grated Cheddar cheese
¼ teaspoon wheat germ
1–2 teaspoons cooked rice
1 eggshell, cooked and finely ground, or 1 pulverized 50-mg calcium tablet

Combine ingredients, form into hamburger patty, and broil until meat is cooked (but not well done). Allow to cool. Cut into bite-size pieces and serve on a people plate. (This makes cats aware of the fact that the meal is a treat and not intended as everyday fare.)

## Questions and Answers About Thirty Days to a Healthier Cat

### MEASURE BY MEASURE

*I still get confused when I have to turn teaspoons into ounces and vice versa. Where can I find a simple guide?*
*Right here:*

|  | VOLUME |  |
|---|---|---|
| 1 quart | = | 4 cups |
|  |  | or |
|  |  | 2 pints |
|  |  | or |
|  |  | 32 fluid ounces |
| 1 cup | = | ½ pint |
| (237 milliliters) |  | or |
|  |  | 8 fluid ounces |
|  |  | or |
|  |  | 16 tablespoons |
| 2 tablespoons | = | 1 fluid ounce |
| (30 milliliters) |  |  |

1 tablespoon      =      3 teaspoons
  (15 milliliters)

| | WEIGHT | |
|---|---|---|
| 28.35 grams | = | 1 ounce |
| 100 grams | = | 3½ ounces |
| 227.8 grams | = | ½ pound (8 ounces) |
| 453.6 grams | = | 1 pound (16 ounces) |

# Special Problems, Special Diets

❖❀❖❀❖❀❖❀

## Allergies

*Allergic reactions vary from cat to cat,
frequently causing confusion.*

An allergy is a hypersensitivity to a specific substance, an allergen, that does not normally cause an unusual reaction (essentially the release of histamine from cells). But allergic reactions, even to the same allergen, can differ from cat to cat (and time to time), depending on an individual animal's type of sensitivity, age, physical condition, and the manner in which contact with the substance was made.

*Reaction Possibilities:* Diarrhea, vomiting, skin lesions, hives, runny eyes, coughing, sneezing, itching, scratching, swelling, dermatitis, hair loss, and more.

*Contact Possibilities:*
• Ingestion (of certain foods, herbs, or medications)
• Inhalation (of pollens, smoke, dust, powders, polishes, feathers, mold)

• Interaction (with certain types of material, dyes, flea collars, powders, soaps)
• Injection (of insect venom [stings], medications)

*Don't Jump to Conclusions:* Before assuming your cat's symptoms are allergic reactions, I'd suggest having your pet checked by a vet to eliminate the possibility of disease or infection. If there is none, and emotional stress due to household tension or environmental change can be ruled out, allergy is a reasonable assumption. The next step is to discover the offending allergen, and the best way is by process of elimination.

### Allergen Elimination Diet

To pinpoint a food allergen, a diet composed of ingredients that the cat hasn't eaten recently or frequently, and that are known for producing allergic response, must be fed exclusively for two weeks. Absolutely no other foods should be given. Only distilled water is allowed for the first two weeks; tap water is recommended as the first dietary addition.

4 ounces boiled lamb or mutton
1 cup long-grain white rice (not "instant" rice), cooked

Chop or grind cooked lamb and combine with rice. Use broth from cooked lamb if a moister meal is preferred. Makes four meals (approximately 125 calories each).

An alternative diet is the Prescription Diet Feline d/d (Hill's), a professional, lamb-based food specifically formulated for diagnosing food-induced allergies. One can supplies five meals (approximately 116 calories each).

If your cat shows improvement after two weeks on this regimen, you can begin adding new foods to the diet, but at the rate of only one ingredient a week. This way, if there's no recurrence of allergic symptoms, you'll know the new food is okay for permanent use in the diet. Begin by adding proteins (beef, liver, poultry, fish, eggs, milk), and then introduce cereal and grain products (oatmeal, cornmeal, barley). Once this is done, find a quality canned or dry food that contains only the ingredients well tolerated by your cat.

If no improvement is shown during the two weeks of the regimen, your cat's problem is evidently not a food allergy, and other possibilities should be investigated, and I'd recommend consulting a board-certified dermatologist. Keep in mind that anything can be an allergen—a hair-ball remedy, a vitamin tablet, a food additive, a cookie, a flea bite—items so seemingly inconsequential that you might never have even considered them. What's important to remember about allergies is that little things do mean a lot—and can do a lot of mean things, especially to susceptible cats.

## Anorexia

*How to give your cat more than a slim chance at renewed health*

Refusal of food for more than two days is abnormal feline behavior. Loss of appetite (anorexia) in cats is always potentially life-threatening and must never be ignored. With this disease, once your pet stops eating, it no longer *wants* to eat, then *won't* eat, and eventually *can't* eat. Whether the cause is emotional (fright, hostility, depression) brought on by a new environment or pet, or physical (pain, injury, trauma) brought on by oral dysfunction, internal obstruction, or illness, the results can be disastrous without quick action and the right nourishment.

*Quick Action for Anorexia:* Bring your cat to a veterinarian as soon as possible. An anorectic cat should not be confused with a finicky eater.

If force-feeding is necessary, follow the basic procedures described in chapter 7 for giving medication. I'd advise obtaining a plastic feeding syringe from your vet or pharmacist. (The 5-ml size is good for cats.)

## The Right Nourishment for an Anorectic Cat

• Water is the most important nutrient and required in the largest amounts. Cats will instinctively cut back on food and physical activity to decrease water loss.

• Increase calorie intake. Though physically inactive, your cat's caloric needs will usually increase in proportion to the severity of the disease or condition responsible for the anorexia.

• Increase protein supply. Protein needs are greater in anorectic cats and must be met with easily digested and utilized high-BV quality sources.

• Provide vitamin and mineral dietary supplements. In the cat's debilitated condition, daily pediatric dosages of zinc, vitamin B complex, and C are recommended.

• Give plenty of stroking and loving. This helps food go down and keeps your cat's spirits up.

## Restarting Stalled Appetites

• Mix one ounce of water with every two to four ounces of a high-fat, easily digestible, calorie-dense (and tasty) professional food, such as canned Prescription Diet Feline p/d (Hill's) or Science Diet Mixit (which is high enough in moisture not to need added water), or add one ounce of sardine or tuna oil to Iams or Feline p/d-dry.

• Feed small amounts four to six times daily.

• Finger-feed (as opposed to force-feed) your cat by placing pill-size portions of food on its tongue.

• Offer baby-food lamb and rice. This is intended *only* as a temporary fast-fix appetite stimulant. After a day or two, the cat should be eased onto a complete nutritionally balanced diet. Gradually replace small portions of the baby food with a quality alternative food. Heating (*not* cooking) the meal will enhance flavor.

## Arthritis

*Cats with a difficult joint problem need salving.*

This painful joint condition is a common affliction of aging cats. Their hindquarters become stiff; movement is difficult; sometimes even waking up seems hard to do. Cortisone drugs will relieve pain, but I feel that unless they're absolutely necessary, a cat is better off without them.

### *Comfort and Nutrition Count*

• Keep the cat in a warm area, away from dampness and drafts.
• Make the litter box easily accessible.
• Feed a quality alternative food with high-BV protein and maximum digestibility.
• Supplement daily diet with the following:
   ¼ teaspoon of brewer's yeast
   100 to 200 mg of vitamin C
   3 to 4 crushed alfalfa tablets
   50 IU of vitamin E
• Do not overfeed. (The last thing an arthritic cat needs to carry around is extra weight.)
CAUTION: Do *not* give aspirin to your cat. It can deprive the blood of oxygen and cause serious respiratory problems, and in some cases, death.

## Cancer

*Not all types are curable, but some are preventable.*

By definition, cancer is a malignant tumor that invades other tissue by metastasis, moving from one part of the body to another, growing on (and destroying) healthy cells by way of the lymphatic system or bloodstream.

*Two Cancer Categories:* Comprising a broad group of malignancies, cancer is divided into two categories: carcinomas and sarcomas. Carcinomas originate in the skin and internal epithelial linings; sarcomas develop from connective tissue—those parts of a cat's body that bind and support it. Within these two categories are numerous types of tumors and malignancies, causes of which are still unknown.

*Preventive Feeding:* There is no cure-all diet for cancer, but a cat with a strong immune system is certainly far better equipped to withstand the rigors of treatment, less likely to succumb to infection during recuperation, and most likely able to spend many more happy years with you.

## Recommended Foods and Supplements

NOTE: If your cat is being treated for cancer or any other illness, do not make any dietary changes or supplement additions without first consulting your vet.

• Quality alternative canned and dry food containing high-BV protein, fat, and numerous vitamins and minerals, as well as ample nondigestible fiber such as beet pulp or whole wheat grains

• 250 to 500 mg of vitamin C daily

• 50 IU of vitamin E daily

• One eighth teaspoon of cod-liver oil daily. (Certain fish oils—cod among them—have recently been found to inhibit growth of tumors in cats.)

• Acidophilus: two tablespoons plain yogurt or one teaspoon Borden's Bene Bac daily

• One quarter teaspoon of brewer's yeast and bran mix added to food once a day

• Nothing that contains sodium nitrite or artificial coloring

No food or supplement regimen is a guarantee against illness, but my New-Life Diet in chapter 10 can offer your cat the best possible chance at good health.

## Diabetes

*Top dietary management is required at all feeding levels.*

When a cat's pancreas fails to produce adequate insulin, the hormone necessary for proper metabolism and maintenance levels of blood sugar (glucose), the result is an improper metabolism of carbohydrates, an uncontrolled rise in blood sugar, and a disease called diabetes mellitus.

In cats, increased thirst and increased urine production are usually the symptoms owners notice first and, thankfully, rarely ignore. Once a diagnosis is made and these cats are put on medication, a strict diabetes management diet, or both, they can live long, happy, active lives.

### Firm Feeding Rules for Your Diabetic Cat

1. In order to establish and maintain a correct insulin dosage, you *must* feed the same amount of food with the same ingredients every day. A fixed-formula food with quality protein, quality-controlled processing, high palatability, and a low carbohydrate content is not an option, it's a necessity.

2. Never make any dietary changes or additions without consulting your veterinarian. Though a diet with more fiber may be healthy for your cat (and high-fiber diets are), a switch could necessitate a reduction of the animal's prescribed insulin dosage—and that's a decision only your pet's doctor is qualified to make.

3. Because virtually all supermarket/commercial-food ingredients vary according to cost and availability, they cannot be relied upon for consistency and thus can undermine the health of an insulin-dependent cat.

4. Feed your cat twice daily, but only high-protein, low-carbohydrate meals, such as Prescription Diet Feline p/d or

c/d (Hill's), Iams (Iams), or Rx Special Diet Formulation N (Cadillac Pet Foods).

5. Once your cat's insulin requirement has been established, maintained, and stabilized, then—and *only* then—can you add a treat food to the diet. But only one! It can be two tablespoons of cottage cheese or one hard-boiled chopped or whole egg yolk (some cats love to roll the whole yolk around and then eat it), but not both! And the one you choose, no other, must be given every day in the same amount until the cat's insulin level is once again checked, established, and stabilized.

CAUTION: Do not add supplements to your cat's food without consulting your vet. Vitamin E can lower insulin requirements, and a combination of thiamine, vitamin C, and cysteine can reduce insulin effectiveness.

*Of course, stopping the disease before it starts is the best way to handle it.*

### Do's and Don'ts for Diabetes Prevention

• *Do* watch your pet's weight. Overweight cats are more prone to diabetes as well as a variety of other ailments.

• *Don't* allow free feeding. (No, Virginia, cats do *not* know when they've had enough.)

• *Do* vary your cat's diet but only with fixed-formula foods.

• *Don't* feed soft-moist food. It's high in sugar and loaded with enough carbohydrates to give an elephant's pancreas a workout.

• *Do* make sure your cat gets plenty of exercise.

• *Don't* feed "people" sweets as treats.

• *Do* add a quarter teaspoon of brewer's yeast and bran mix to meals, and be sure your cat's getting its full zinc requirement daily.

## Fleas

*No fleas, please!*

A flea can be a lot more than a little pest. These are hardy villains and can live for up to three years on a cat. They can cause allergies, parasite infections, skin conditions, and more. They should be kept out of your home and off your pet. Ask your vet for a flea collar and an insecticide with pyrethrins; carboyl is not as effective.

*Feed for Protection:* Add a quarter teaspoon of brewer's yeast to your cat's breakfast and dinner every day. The B vitamins—thiamine, in particular—cause the cat's skin to give off sulfur, *which works as a natural insect repellent.*

## Feline Leukemia (FeLV)

*Some cats are carriers, others are victims, but all are potential targets for this cancerous virus.*

Highly contagious, this feline viral blood cancer is spread through the saliva (possibly also the urine and feces) of infected cats. Once the disease is contracted, a cat generally does not survive for more than several months, despite medical treatment.

The symptoms—jaundice, anemia, weight loss, appetite loss, diarrhea or constipation, enlarged lymph nodes, fatigue, excessive thirst and/or urination, respiratory distress, infertility, and more—also include a deteriorating immunity that prevents victims from warding off other disease. As yet there is no cure, but one vaccine, Leukocell, is available, though I wouldn't recommend it for any but high-risk cats, since its safety and effectiveness are still being questioned. Other vaccines are now being tested, and approval of them for general veterinary use is expected soon.

*Feeding for Fortification:* A healthy adult cat, exposed to the virus, can develop immunity to the primary disease (in effect, suppress it) and live out a normal life. But should this carrier's natural defenses be nutritionally let down, particularly during a period of stress, the disease could then surface and strike. By having your cat tested for FeLV annually, you can keep a check on its immune system, adjust changing nutrient needs accordingly, and prevent the possibility of making an unwise medical decision for your pet that you might regret for the rest of your life.

### Recipe for Resistance

• Vary feeding of canned and dry foods that contain high-BV protein in a good ratio to quality fat, an impressive vitamin-mineral assay, no artificial coloring or sodium nitrite or more than one preservative.
• One quarter teaspoon of brewer's yeast and bran mix added to one meal daily
• One eighth teaspoon wheat germ oil mixed with food three to five times weekly
• 50 to 100 mg of vitamin C daily
• Balanced fatty-acid supplement with zinc five times weekly
• Contents of one capsule of bee pollen mixed with food daily
• 25 to 50 mg of vitamin E three to five times weekly

## FUS (Feline Urologic Syndrome)

*If you own a cat, don't think about FUS—*
*do something about it.*

Feline urologic syndrome (FUS) is one of the most common and painful cat ailments, sending thousands of cats a year to veterinary hospitals and probably an equal number of owners up the wall. Ironically, it's one of the most preventable feline problems.

Characterized by frequent strained voiding of small quantities of odorous, often bloody, urine in locations other than the litter box, FUS is essentially caused by the presence of struvite (magnesium crystals) and calculi in the urinary tract, where they can promote obstruction, serious urethral irritation, and dangerous blockage.

### Avoiding and Treating FUS

• Feed a diet low in magnesium and high in calories. The greater a food's caloric density, the less a cat needs to consume. This decreases magnesium intake and thereby its presence in the urine.

• Keep the litter box clean and provide fresh water daily. No hard water, please. It usually contains too much magnesium for a cat's comfort.

• No free feeding, and only two meals a day. After eating, urine acidity decreases, and calculi formation can increase. You want *acidic* urine. Fewer feedings per day help keep FUS away.

• Be wary of supermarket/commercial "low ash" foods. Ash is the residue of many minerals your cat *needs*. What you want to know is the level of *magnesium* in that ash, which your cat *doesn't need*. For prevention of calculi formation, you want foods to contain less than 1 percent—dry matter basis—with a calcium/phosphorus ratio of 1.2:1.

• Feed only foods with high-BV protein (meat, poultry, fish, eggs) that usually produce acidic urine. Other proteins, such as soybean meal, wheat middlings, corn gluten meal, and so on, generally do not produce acidic urine, and they rank pretty low on my nutritional scale, too.

• Encourage increased liquid intake. Sneak a tablespoon or two of water, broth, or tomato juice into all canned meals. If necessary, and sodium is not restricted, you can probably get your cat to drink without having to lead it to water by adding a pinch of salt to its food.

• Avoid high-magnesium treats, such as shrimp or nuts, and feed only foods that are acceptable for FUS management.

• Don't add brewer's yeast (0.17 percent magnesium) to food if your cat has an FUS problem. (Dietary management of cystitis, inflammation of the bladder, and urolithiasis, inflammation or blockage of the urethra, is basically the same as for FUS.)

## Heart Disease

*Where the heart is concerned, a cat is never too old or too young to have problems.*

Cardiovascular ailments can afflict cats of all ages. Though there is a wide variety of heart problems, differing in severity and symptoms (which range from simple weakness, mild coughing, insomnia, and weight loss to labored breathing, excessive thirst and urination, abdominal distension and collapse), all are cause for concern and treatment.

The proper functioning of a cat's vital organs, particularly the kidneys' capacity to filter out and excrete waste, depends on the health of the cardiovascular system. And in order to retain and restore this health, dietary management is essential.

*Pass on the Salt:* Reducing the cat's intake of sodium is of primary importance, since salt causes water retention. Water retention puts a heavier load on kidneys already overworked and underfueled because of impaired cardiac function and can result in heart failure.

### Knowing the Right "No's" for the Heart

• No smoked food or any luncheon meats. Also nix on shellfish, canned soups, foods with monosodium glutamate

(MSG, Accent), processed cheeses, breads and cereals, canned vegetables, and people food in general.

• No cat foods that list salt as an ingredient. (Commercial cat food ingredients already contain salt, so an additional listing means there's much more in there than your cat can handle safely.)

• No protein other than that of the highest utilizable quality. You don't want any more waste material going through the kidneys than necessary, and you do want your pet to get the best amino acids possible.

• No water treated by a home water softener. Home water softeners add sodium. If you are unsure about the sodium content of your tap water, provide distilled water and encourage your pet to drink.

• No added supplements if you are feeding your pet a prescription diet, such as Feline h/d, Feline k/d, or Feline c/d-dry (Hill's) or Rx Special Diet Formulation H (Cadillac). Prescription diets are carefully formulated, and supplement additions, with the exception of brewer's yeast (which is advised because of its B vitamins and antistress properties), can undermine the nutrient ratio designed to maintain a correct electrolyte balance.

### A Few Heart-to-Heart Tips and Cautions

• If your cat is overweight, decrease portion sizes of its low-salt meals. Unless specifically prescribed, avoid feeding prepared reducing diets, since they are usually high in salt.

• Sometimes a cat is mistakenly thought obese when the problem is actually edema, a condition in which the cat's body tissues contain an excessive amount of fluid. Edema causes the animal to appear fat when in fact it's much too thin. If this is the case, a half tablespoon of corn oil can be added to each low-salt meal, along with a small (quarter ounce) portion of meat.

• Chopped cucumbers are natural diuretics, which increase urine excretion, and can be added to food.

• If you are not feeding a prescription low-sodium food, supplement the cat's diet with a balanced 50-mg vitamin B complex with C daily, and 50 IU of vitamin E five days a week.

• If you are preparing homemade meals, do not use baking soda as an ingredient.

• For finicky eaters, see how to make the switch to a new food in chapter 10.

• Exercise is important, but consult your vet on how much your cat is allowed.

## DR. JANE'S *SANS*-SALT SUPPER

*A homemade meal that your cat can enjoy
to its heart's delight*

4 ounces cooked ground beef
1 ounce cooked beef liver
¼ cup cooked (without salt) long-grain white rice (not "instant" rice)
¼ teaspoon corn oil
¼ teaspoon calcium carbonate or other calcium supplement without sodium (available at health food stores and pharmacies)
¼ teaspoon brewer's yeast
1 thin slice cucumber, finely chopped

Braise beef and liver in small amount of unsalted water in a covered saucepan. Cook 5–10 minutes, depending upon whether your pet prefers meat rare, medium, or well done. Chop liver into tiny chunks. Transfer cooked beef and liver to feeding dish and mix in remaining ingredients. Add as much cooking liquid as needed to achieve desired consistency. Test food to see that it's cooled to room temperature before serving.

### Kidney Disease

*Not all old cats have it, and many young ones do.*

One of the most widely propagated health myths about cats—which many vets continue to believe—is that if they're old and they're sick they have kidney disease. And this just isn't true! Granted, as cats age, there is a gradual, natural deceleration of kidney function, but this is not kidney disease! And considering the abundance of inferior protein being foisted on cats these days, it's remarkable that it isn't.

The kidneys, which are responsible for gathering and distributing needed nutrients and eliminating harmful substances from the blood, spend most of their time excreting waste from nutrient breakdown. This means that the less quality a protein has, the more work the kidneys must do. Conversely, more quality protein means less work for the kidneys.

*Owner Alert:* Kidney disease symptoms (scratching, mangy coat, fatigue, increased thirst, frequent urination), indicative as they might appear, are not proof of the disease. Without a BUN (blood, urea, nitrogen concentration) test to determine the levels at which the kidneys are functioning, no accurate diagnosis can be made.

Because the disease can strike cats of all ages, I recommend that your pet be given a BUN test annually, especially after the age of six. The earlier that potential problems are detected, the easier the disease is to prevent.

### Prevention Is as Easy as 1-2-3

1. Switch your pet to a high-BV-protein alternative food and serve it only twice daily, unless contraindicated because of pregnancy, surgery, medication, or other special circumstance.

2. If the cat is overweight, it's instant shape-up time. (See section on obesity below.)

3. Supplement its diet with:

One quarter teaspoon of brewer's yeast twice daily with food
100 to 200 mg of vitamin C daily
Plenty of fresh water daily

## What to Do If Your Cat Has Kidney Problems

If a BUN test shows that your cat has a kidney disease, or renal damage that has impaired proper kidney function, you must pay *strict* attention to special nutritional guidelines.

• Protein intake must be restricted and limited to highest quality sources; the extent of protein limitation is determined by how effectively and at what level the kidneys are functioning.

• Sodium intake must be restricted. (See suggestions in "Heart Disease" section above.)

• Phosphorus intake must be restricted. Avoid foods with an inverse calcium/phosphorus ratio. (See chapter 4.)

• Provide professional, fixed-formula food with restricted high-quality protein and minerals, such as Prescription Diet Feline k/d or c/d-dry (Hill's) or Rx Special Diet Formulation H (Cadillac).

## Liver (Hepatic) Disease

*Even a cat with nine lives has only one liver, and it's vital that you know how to care for it.*

The liver is your pet's frontline fighter against invading poisons, pathogens, and toxins; the engineer in charge of storing and efficiently dispensing fat, fat-soluble vitamins, and glycogen; the provider of blood-clotting vitamin K; the force behind effective carbohydrate, fat, and protein metabolism, bile production, and more. Needless to say, when this organ becomes diseased, your cat's life depends on its recovery.

*Multiple Symptoms and Causes:* Lethargy, weight loss, anemia, jaundice, diarrhea, and vomiting are only a few of the numerous distress signals indicating liver trouble. Liver trouble can stem from an equally large number of causes and is therefore one of the few diseases more difficult to prevent than to treat, which is why understanding the management of this ailment is so important.

### Get-Well Notes to Remember

1. Feed your pet restricted amounts of thoroughly digestible, utilizable, high-BV protein, but *not a high-protein diet*. This might sound contradictory, but it's not. The point is to reduce the liver's workload—which involves removal of waste from amino acids—and provide relief for the kidneys, while still supplying quality protein needed for recovery.

2. If your pet has no appetite, follow the advice given in the section on anorexia above, but do not feed baby food. Baby food hasn't enough of the necessary balanced protein, fat, minerals, and vitamins, and often too much phosphorus. Prescription Diet Feline k/d (Hill's) is properly formulated for liver ailments and can be made into a liquid preparation by adding distilled water.

3. Salt and phosphorus intake should be restricted. (More relief for the kidneys, which have no choice but to be involved when there's liver trouble.)

4. Equal parts of cottage cheese and cooked brown rice are highly digestible and work well as a diet in the early stages of the illness. A soft-boiled egg (or raw egg yolk) mixed in adds palatability. This should not be used as an extended, long-term diet, since it doesn't contain the proper balance of necessary vitamins and minerals, but it can be added anytime to a prescription diet that needs a flavor booster.

5. Add no additional fats to food, and give *no fat-soluble vitamins*. (Again, too much work for the liver.)

6. Keep methionine and choline *out* of the diet. The intestines will convert these into mercaptans, which are toxic, and with the liver unable to oust them from the body, encephalopathy, a dysfunctioning of the brain, can occur.

7. Feed small amounts of food four to six times daily. This gives the debilitated liver a chance to relax between workloads.

8. B vitamins, with the exception of choline, are recommended as daily supplements. The B's are stress fighters. If using a vitamin $B_1$, $B_2$, and $B_6$ combination, be sure they're given together in equal dosage. Too much of one can deplete the others. A daily dosage of 50 mg is fine.

9. Restrict foods with fish meal, melts (spleens of slaughtered animals), and other glandular products, shellfish, and meats. The liver is in no condition to handle their wastes, which can cause an unwanted buildup of uric acid.

10. When adding carbohydrates to the diet, use easily digestible buckwheat groats (kasha), oatmeal, or cornmeal (polenta). Only add carbohydrates if your cat is getting enough protein. Do not use whole corn, which is hard to digest.

## Obesity

*With the exception of Garfield, it's no fun*
*for a cat to be fat.*

Some cats are naturally round and puffy-looking; others are naturally lean and muscular (see chapter 6 for descriptions of different breeds). But no cat is naturally fat.

You should suspect that your cat is overweight if its abdomen and/or chest sags; if it has difficulty grooming itself; if you try to feel its rib cage and can't; or if you have to pinch the flesh along its backbone more than an inch to find it.

You should *know* that it is overweight if you say, "Here, kitty, kitty," and then feel the house shake, can't see its paws, or find it needs a forklift to get into the litter box. Because if you don't, you're both in BIG trouble.

A cat that's overweight can develop serious problems. Once excess pounds pile on, normal exercise and movement slack off, along with daily hygiene. Twisting its body to wash the hindquarters or genital area becomes increasingly difficult, and eventually the animal gives up. Before long, the result of neglect becomes visible: dull hair becomes matted and sparse, and small lesions provide moist havens for bacteria, turning minor skin irritations into persistent infections. And this is only the beginning.

## Weighty Problems for Overweight Cats

### DIABETES

The more a cat eats, the higher its blood sugar, the more insulin it needs, and the harder its pancreas has to work. Without a change of pace—or diet—insulin cells burn out and diabetes set in.

### HEART AND LIVER DISEASES

Fat doesn't accumulate only in visible areas, but also around the heart and liver. The former decreases blood flow to organs and causes numerous cardiovascular as well as respiratory problems; the latter creates serious digestive disorders and a conglomeration of interrelated illnesses.

### DECREASED RESISTANCE TO INFECTION

Extra weight overworks all vital organs, stresses the body, depletes nutrients, weakens the immune system, and prevents efficient production of protective antibodies.

## Ounce-for-Ounce, Pound-for-Pound Prevention

Feline obesity occurs when a cat's calorie intake exceeds its bodily needs and daily energy expenditure. This *could* be caused by hypothyroidism, which slows down the metabolism rate at which calories are normally consumed, but it's usually not. *Obesity is a preventable disease, and it's up to you to prevent it!*

• Determine what your cat should weigh, then feed it only enough calories to maintain that weight. (See chapter 3.)

• Don't get in the habit of creating bad habits, such as giving between-meal snacks; offering food from the table just because you happen to be eating at the moment and your pet isn't; using food as a reward; or providing an assortment of meals for your finicky eater (who'll end up eating more than a fair share of all of them).

• Know the approximate calories of foods you feed, and avoid those high in carbohydrates and sugar.

• Substitute vegetables for high-calorie commercial snacks.

• Don't leave food down for more than twenty minutes. A cat that's allowed to eat whenever it wants will get into the habit of eating more often—and more than it should.

• Don't use milk as a substitute for water.

• Play with your pet often. A cat kept on its paws is easier to keep in shape.

• Don't keep your house too warm. It tends to make cats lazy, less active, and larger.

• If your cat is a competitive eater, feed away from other animals or at another time.

• Use your eyes and your head about feeding. If your cat looks as if it's gaining weight, cut back on the portion size. It's as simple as that. Unless you've let things go too far and have to put your cat on a real diet, just reduce the amount of food *gradually.* That's only fair. After all, you're the one who should have been counting the calories.

### When It's Time to Diet

If your cat is overweight and you must put it on a diet, my advice is to get a professional reducing food, such as Prescription Diet Feline r/d (Hill's). It's high in fiber and provides enough bulk to satisfy a cat used to eating a substantial quantity of food.

If you're restricting your pet's total food intake, remember that it means you're restricting intake of necessary vitamins and minerals, too. A balanced vitamin-mineral supplement (such as Fauve or Vital Nutrition) should be given daily. I'd also suggest 50 mg of vitamin B complex with C once a day to reduce stress.

## Worms (Intestinal Parasites)

*Once they're in your cat, they can take a lot out of it.*

If your cat spends time outdoors, and is the sort unlikely to pass up any recreational eating that's within paw's reach, chances are it has worms. By no means does this imply that you're to rush out for medicine and immediately worm your pet. In fact, I strongly caution *against* doing so.

No worm medication should ever be given to a cat before a diagnosis has been made by a veterinarian, especially since the general symptoms of parasite infestation (vomiting, diarrhea, grass eating, fatigue, dull coat, runny eyes, weight loss) could be indicators of numerous diseases. Furthermore, over-the-counter worm medication can be extremely harmful to many cats; if improperly administered or given under the wrong circumstances, it could be lethal. *Never worm a kitten or a cat that's pregnant, nursing, sick, or geriatric without professional supervision.*

The most common intestinal parasites are roundworms, hookworms, tapeworms, and whipworms. Roundworms are frequently passed from an infected queen to her kittens. Tapeworms are usually contracted by cats that have eaten fleas, whose primary diet is tapeworm eggs. Decayed food, feces, stagnant water, and insects are breeding grounds for these parasites; field mice, birds, moles, and rabbits are common carriers. Any outdoor cat that escapes infestation is either pretty lucky or lying.

Nutrition is your cat's best protection:
• Feed the optimal New-Life Diet (chapter 10).
• Supplement all meals with a quarter teaspoon of brewer's yeast (unless your pet has an FUS problem).
• Give 50 mg of vitamin C daily.

## *If Your Cat Has Worms*

• Until your cat is free of infestation, feed it a high-carbohy-drate—not necessarily high-protein—diet. The digestible portion of carbohydrates will provide nutrients for your cat, leaving the nondigestible surplus in the intestines to feed the worms. If only protein enters the intestines, the worms—not your cat—get the nutrients.

• Add bread to food (a thin slice, crumbled, and mixed with meals).

• Divide food into three or four meals daily. A large protein-rich meal could send hungry worms into a frenzy that might be lethal for your pet.

• Give a balanced vitamin-mineral supplement daily.

• An additional 50 mg of vitamin B complex and 150 mg of vitamin C should be given once or twice daily, for stress, until your cat is worm-free.

## Questions and Answers About Special Problems and Special Diets

### NONESSENTIALS ABOUT NEUTERING

*Will neutering my cats make them more vulnerable to obesity and FUS?*

Neutering a cat, male or female, will generally cause a decrease in physical activity, which can predispose the cat to obesity and FUS, if dietary precautions are not taken. But if you take these precautions and encourage exercise, a neutered cat is no more vulnerable than one that is not.

### MURMURS ARE MEANINGFUL

*My seven-year-old male (a domestic shorthair) has a heart murmur. My vet told me that it was nothing to worry about, but I do. Am I overreacting?*

I don't think you're overreacting, and I think it is important that you put your pet on a low-sodium diet immediately. Heart murmurs in cats are frequently early warning signs of more serious cardiovascular problems, so why take a chance? Follow the dietary cautions given in the "Heart Disease" section above—then you and your pet can both relax.

## ALLERGY VS. INTOLERANCE

*My cat has been diagnosed as having a milk intolerance. Is there any difference between an intolerance and an allergy? And if so, what is it?*

Yes, there is a difference. Let me start by saying that most adverse reactions evidenced in adult cats are due to milk intolerance; this is an intolerance of lactose (milk sugar), caused by an insufficiency of the digestive enzyme lactase. A milk *allergy,* on the other hand, is a hypersensitivity to the protein in milk.

With a lactose intolerance, your cat is usually still able to eat cheese, butter, foods containing dried milk, and other dairy products with no ill effects. With a milk allergy, all forms have to be eliminated from the diet. Any cat food containing whey or casein, for example, cannot be fed. I should add that it's not uncommon for cats allergic to milk to also react adversely to beef.

## THE ITCH-SCRATCH-ITCH SYNDROME

*I've been told that my cat Murray (an eight-year-old neutered male shorthair) has neurological dermatitis. I don't quite understand what this is, and why it keeps recurring. I'd greatly appreciate a simple explanation and any suggestions you might have for treatment.*

I wish there were a simple explanation, but because every cat is an individual, there isn't. Neurological dermatitis is a condition in which an animal licks, scratches, or bites itself in a specific region for no apparent reason. This usually results in a secondary infection, which causes more itching and scratching, subsequently establishing a vicious cycle.

There are cortisone drugs that can alleviate itching and clear up infection, but cats, being creatures of habit, often resume this self-destructive behavior, possibly when under stress or if subjected to whatever irritant might have initiated the condition, thereby restarting the cycle. Though neurological dermatitis can be cured temporarily, it remains a lifetime condition and can reappear at any time. Antihistamines, such as Chlor-Trimeton, are helpful, but should only be given under veterinary advice. *Do not* give your cat aspirin; the consequences could be lethal.

Fortifying Murray with stress-fighting B complex vitamins and wound-healing vitamins C, A, and E and zinc, along with a high-BV-protein, quality-fat diet, is your best preventive and defense for his condition.

# Where to Find Help

✦✿✦✿✦✿✦✿

## Organizations and Information Sources

*When you have questions and need answers, it's good to know where to get them.*

American Society for the Prevention of Cruelty to Animals (ASPCA)
441 East 92nd Street
New York, NY 10128

Offers information about spay/neuter programs, shelters, adoption services, and humane education.

American Veterinary Holistic Medical Association
2214 Old Emmorton Road
Bel Air, MD 21014

Provides information about holistic medical treatments for cats.

American Veterinary Medical Association
930 North Meacham Road
Schaumburg, IL 60196

> Provides information about locating local veterinarians and board-certified specialists; also handles complaints about animal medical treatments and questions about cat health in general.

Animal Toxicology Hot Line (217) 333-3611

> Round-the-clock, seven-day-a-week service for information and advice about suspected or known cases of cat poisoning or chemical contamination.

Cornell Feline Health Center
Attention: Fredric W. Scott, D.V.M., Ph.D.
College of Veterinary Medicine
Cornell University
Ithaca, NY 14853

> Provides information about the latest research in feline nutrition and diseases.

Friends of Animals, Inc.
Attention: Harrison Maas, Esq.
One Pine Street
Neptune, NJ 07753

> Subsidizes spay and neutering programs.

The Humane Society of the United States
Attention: John A. Hoyt
2100 L Street, N.W.
Washington, DC 20037

> Through educational programs and lobbying, supports humane treatment of all living things.

Life Extension Foundation
    2835 Hollywood Boulevard
    Hollywood, FL 33020

    Can supply information on feline longevity nutrition.

Morris Animal Foundation
    45 Inverness Drive East
    Englewood, CO 80112

    Researches and can provide information on feline diseases; also will supply a nutrition bulletin by Dr. Lon Lewis on request. (Send self-addressed, stamped envelope.)

Robert H. Winn Foundation for Cat Research
    1309 Allaire Avenue
    Ocean, NJ 07712

    Researches and can provide information on feline diseases.

# Glossary
# of Abbreviations

◊❀◊❀◊❀◊❀

**AAFCO.** Association of American Feed Control Officials; animal feed control officials from the United States and Canada who develop and enforce laws and regulations for the production of animal feed and pet food; responsible for enforcing truth in pet food labeling.

**BHA.** A preservative and antioxidant; used in most cat foods to prevent spoilage of oils and fats; can be toxic to the kidneys, but is generally considered to be less so than BHT.

**BHT.** A preservative and antioxidant used to prevent spoilage of fats and oils; present in many cat foods; generally considered to be more toxic to the kidneys than its chemical cousin BHA.

**BUN.** Blood, urea, nitrogen concentration test for kidney ailments.

**BV.** Biological value; the percentage of a nutrient absorbed, retained, and therefore presumably utilized by the cat's body.

**FDA.** Food and Drug Administration.

**FIP.** Feline infectious peritonitis; a viral cat disease that grows in white cells and circulates throughout the body; when cells are destroyed they release toxins; contagious; uncommon; usually fatal.

**FUS.** Feline urologic syndrome; a common lower urinary tract condition characterized by frequent strained voiding of small

239

amounts of urine that is often bloody; a blockage of the urinary tract primarily from a buildup of mineral crystals. Also known as cystitis urolithiasis.

**GRAS.** "Generally recognized as safe"; a list established by the U.S. Congress to cover substances added to food.

**IU.** International units.

**NRC.** The National Academy of Science's National Research Council, whose subcommittee on cat nutrition is composed of veterinary nutritionists who meet, examine, and update nutritional requirements every several years.

**PUFA.** Polyunsaturated fatty acid.

**RDA.** Recommended dietary allowances as established by the Food and Nutrition Board, National Academy of Sciences.

# Recommended Reading for Cat Owners

The books listed here are among those that have provided me with many hours of pleasure and knowledge, and I hope that they'll do the same for you. Some simply afford amusement, others are for reference and advice, but all are for encouraging new discoveries in the endlessly fascinating world of cats.

*The Book of the Cat*, by Michael Wright and Sally Walters. New York: Summit Books, 1982.

*Common Sense Book of Complete Cat Care*, by Louis L. Vine. New York: Warner Books, 1978.

*Dr. Pitcairn's Complete Guide to Natural Health for Dogs and Cats*, by Richard H. Pitcairn and Susan Hubble Pitcairn. Emmaus, Pa.: Rodale Press, 1982.

*Dog and Cat Good Food Book*, by Terri McGinnis. New York: Random House, 1977.

*Harper's Illustrated Handbook of Cats*, edited by Roger Caras. New York: Harper & Row, 1985.

*The Healthy Cat and Dog Book*, by Joan Harper. New York: E. P. Dutton, 1979.

*The Kitty-Cat Cookbook*, by Barbara Ellen Benson. Los Angeles: Barrington Productions, 1983.

*The Natural History of Cats*, by Claire Necker. New York: Dell Publishing, 1970.

*No Nàughty Cats: The First Guide to Intelligent Cat Training*, by Debra Pirotin, D.V.M., and Sherry Suib Cohen. New York: Harper & Row, 1985.

*The Simple, Plain and Different Cookbook for Cats*, by Jacqueline Russel. Rochester, N.Y.: Russel Press, 1983.

*Travel with Your Pet*, by Paula Weideger and Geraldine Thorsten. New York: Simon & Schuster, 1973.

*Understanding Your Cat*, by Michael W. Fox. New York: Coward, McCann & Geoghegan, 1974.

*The Very Healthy Cat Book*, by Wendell O. Belfield and Martin Zucker. New York: McGraw-Hill, 1983.

*What to Do till the Veterinarian Comes*, by Jean Pommery. Opéra Mundi, 1973. English translation and final chapter by Chilton Book Company, Radnor, Pa., 1976.

*Wholly Cats*, by Faith McNulty and Elisabeth Keiffer. Indianapolis: Bobbs-Merrill, 1962.

# Index

o☸o☸o☸o☸